T0326942

"From its first word the Gospel of John calls its readers to the Word—and not just the Word, his life and actions, but the word of the Word, the revelation of God to people. Bruce Schuchard's *The Word from the Beginning* zeroes in on this cardinal motif as he explains how the speech of Jesus shapes his actions as well as those around him. I heartily recommend *The Word from the Beginning* as an aid to hear the word of the Word in John's Gospel—a word we must hear and embrace."

DOUGLAS ESTES,

associate professor of biblical studies and practical theology, Tabor College; editor, *Didaktikos*

"Reading John's Gospel around the central theme of the Word, Bruce Schuchard shows how God's communication informs each part of the narrative that follows. His text is theologically rich and invites readers into deeper reflection about the significance of the Word that Jesus embodies and conveys. Clear and accessible, this volume will appeal to a broad audience, offering insights useful for preaching and study."

CRAIG KOESTER,

Asher O. and Carrie Nasby professor of New Testament, Luther Seminary

"One must hear the Word of God in order to see and believe in him. This is the heart of Schuchard's theological reading of the Gospel of John. In this short expository commentary of the Gospel of John, Schuchard guides readers through the Gospel story, inviting them to hear the Word anew, by providing expository comments and unobtrusive evidence from his own research. Focusing on the Prologue's characterization of Jesus as the Word made Flesh, Schuchard demonstrates how the Gospel of John incorporates this identity into Jesus's person and work from the beginning of his signs to his final farewell in John 21. For Schuchard, those who relegate Jesus's identity as the Word to only the Prologue miss out on the full profundity of the Gospel's message. Schuchard's work shows the fruit of his characteristic care in exploring the use of the Old Testament in John, offering immersive explanations of debated passages. Readers will enjoy Schuchard's poetic and inviting style that makes this book ideal for congregational settings and devotional reading."

ALICIA D. MYERS,

associate professor, New Testament and Greek, Campbell University Divinity School

"Bruce Schuchard has written a beautiful little book that is succinct, insightful, and imminently readable. Schuchard's deep understanding of the Fourth Gospel is obvious on every page, as he guides his readers through the unfolding story of the Word made flesh. After you read this book, you will want to buy a dozen copies to give as gifts to family and friends."

CRAIG A. EVANS,
John Bisagno Distinguished Professor of Christian Origins,
Houston Baptist University

The
WORD
from the
BEGINNING

Bruce G. Schuchard

The
WORD
from the
BEGINNING

The **Person** *and* **Work** *of* **Jesus**
in the **Gospel** *of* **John**

Bruce G. Schuchard

LEXHAM
ACADEMIC

The Word from the Beginning: The Person and Work of Jesus in the Gospel of John

Copyright 2022 Bruce G. Schuchard

Lexham Academic, an imprint of Lexham Press
1313 Commercial St., Bellingham, WA 98225
LexhamPress.com

Print ISBN 9781683596028
Digital ISBN 9781683596103
Library of Congress Control Number 2022933922

Lexham Editorial: Derek Brown, Jeff Reimer, Kelsey Matthews, Mandi Newell
Cover Design: Brittany Schrock
Typesetting: Danielle Thevenaz

COLLECT *for the* WORD
or COLLECT *for the* SECOND SUNDAY *in* ADVENT

In the name of the Father and of the Son and of the Holy Spirit.
Amen.

Teach me Your way, O LORD, that I may walk in Your truth. *Psalm 86:11*
Your Word is a lamp to my feet and a light to my path. *Psalm 119:105*

Blessed LORD,
You have caused all holy Scriptures to be written for our learning:
Grant that we may so hear them, read, mark, learn, and inwardly digest them,
that by patience and comfort of Your holy word,
we may embrace and ever hold fast the blessed hope of everlasting life,
which You have given us in our Savior Jesus Christ.
Amen.

CONTENTS

ABBREVIATIONS

AB	Anchor Bible
ACCS	Ancient Christian Commentary on Scripture
Adv. haer.	*Adversus haereses* (Irenaeus)
ANF	*The Ante-Nicene Fathers.* Edited by Alexander Roberts and James Donaldson. 1885–1887. 10 vols. Repr., Peabody, MA: Hendrickson, 1994.
Ant.	*Antiquities of the Jews* (Josephus)
ANTC	Abingdon New Testament Commentaries
ASBT	Acadia Studies in Bible and Theology
AusBR	*Australian Biblical Review*
BDAG	Danker, Frederick W., Walter Bauer, William F. Arndt, and F. Wilbur Gingrich. *Greek-English Lexicon of the New Testament and Other Early Christian Literature.* 3rd ed. Chicago: University of Chicago Press, 2000
BECNT	Baker Exegetical Commentary on the New Testament
BETL	Bibliotheca Ephemeridum Theologicarum Lovaniensium
BibInt	Biblical Interpretation Series
BNTC	Black's New Testament Commentaries
CBQ	*Catholic Biblical Quarterly*
ConcC	Concordia Commentaries
COQG	Christian Origins and the Question of God
Decal.	*De decalogo* (Philo)
Det.	*Quod deterius potiori insidari soleat* (Philo)
Deus	*Quod Deus sit immutabilis* (Philo)
Did.	Didache
Eccles. Rab.	Ecclesiastes Rabbah
ExpTim	*Expository Times*
FC	Fathers of the Church

Fug.	*De fuga et inventione* (Philo)
IVPNTC	InterVarsity Press New Testament Commentary
JBL	*Journal of Biblical Literature*
JETS	*Journal of the Evangelical Society*
JSNT	*Journal for the Study of the New Testament*
JSNTSup	Journal for the Study of the New Testament Supplement Series
Lev. Rab.	Leviticus Rabbah
LNTS	Library of New Testament Studies
LW	*Luther's Works* [= "American Edition"]. 82 vols. planned. St. Louis: Concordia; Philadelphia: Fortress, 1955–1986; 2009–.
LXX	Septuagint
m. Ketub.	Mishnah tractate of the Ketubbot
m. Yebam.	Mishnah tractate of the Yebamot
MT	Masoretic Text
Mut.	*De mutatione nominum* (Philo)
NTD	Neue Testament Deutsch
NIBCNT	New International Biblical Commentary on the New Testament
NICNT	New International Commentary on the New Testament
NovTSup	Supplements to Novum Testamentum
NTL	New Testament Library
PNTC	Pillar New Testament Commentaries
RBS	Resources for Biblical Study
SBLDS	Society for Biblical Literature Dissertation Series
Sem.	Semaḥot
Sib. Or.	Sibylline Oracles
SNTSMS	Society of New Testament Studies Monograph Series
Somn.	*De somniis* (Philo)
SP	Sacra Pagina
Spec. Laws	On the Special Laws (Philo)
sys	Syrus Sinaiticus
WPC	Westminster Pelican Commentaries
WUNT	Wissenschaftliche Untersuchungen zum Neuen Testament

INTRODUCTION

D oes the Gospel of John's initial manner of repeatedly referring to Jesus as "the Word"[1] sharply distinguish its Prologue from the rest of the Gospel of John?[2] Did the Prologue exist first as an independent Logos hymn? Is its first interest nowhere to be found in the rest of the Gospel of John? What follows will argue that the answer to all these questions is no. Specifically, it will contend that those who say such things[3] fail to account for the *person* and the *work* of the Word Made Flesh.

The Gospel speaks with great frequency of the *word* of the Word Made Flesh.[4] In its Prologue, it is keen first to establish *who the Word is*. In what follows, it is equally keen to establish *what the Word does*. For he comes from a God whose "very being is one of speaking and communication."[5] He comes from him whose Word the Word is. And he speaks. He speaks *a word that must be heard*. That Prologue and narrative are linked in this way

---

1. See "In the beginning was the Word, and the Word was with God, and the Word was God" in 1:1; and "the Word became flesh" in 1:14. See also "concerning the Word of Life" in 1 John 1:1; and "the name by which he is called is the Word of God" in Revelation 19:13.

2. For an earlier form of these introductory paragraphs, see Bruce G. Schuchard, "The Gospel of John and the Word of the Word-Made-Flesh," *Didaktikos* 1 (January 2018): 45.

3. For the range of what has been recently proposed, see Jan G. van der Watt, R. Alan Culpepper, and Udo Schnelle, eds., *The Prologue of the Gospel of John: Its Literary, Theological, and Philosophical Contexts* (Tübingen: Mohr Siebeck, 2016).

4. Ed. L. Miller marks well the Evangelist's "penchant for the word 'word,' and specifically the frequency with which he employs it in relation to his presentation of the activity and teaching of Jesus," in "The Johannine Origins of the Johannine Logos," *JBL* 112 (1993): 451. The Evangelist speaks in many and various ways of the words of Jesus "of keeping the Word, of hearing the Word, of abiding in the Word, and of the Word of him who sent Jesus" (William C. Weinrich, *John 1:1–7:1*, ConcC [St. Louis: Concordia, 2015], 185).

5. Weinrich, *John 1:1–7:1*, 134. Thus, the Prologue's very first verse describes "the eternal existence of the Word as Speech from God: the Word *is* in that God speaks his Word. The 'essence' (οὐσία) of God (to use a traditional ontological category) is a Speaking" (126). The "beginning" of which verse 1 of the Prologue speaks is therefore also "neither void nor abstract. It is filled with the Word, and that necessarily includes also the One whose Word the Word is."

is supported in every way "by the basic Johannine thought that Jesus not only *brings* revelation, but in his person *is* revelation."[6]

Who is the God of the Gospel of John? And how is God known when he is "from above" and we are "from below" (8:23)? How can he be known when we are of this world and he is not? In the Gospel of John, there is more to Jesus than meets the eye. Jesus comes to make known the God that no one has ever seen (1:18). But the God that no one has ever seen can only be seen by the one who sees Jesus as he must be seen (12:45; 14:6, 9, 21). And the seeing of Jesus as he must be seen can only be done by the one who *takes him at his word* (5:24; 8:31, 43, 51; 12:47–50; 14:23–24). Only ears can tell you what your eyes cannot. Only the one who hears Jesus sees Jesus.[7] Only the one who sees Jesus sees God.

A comprehensive thematic reading of the Gospel of John will show that the Gospel's pronounced interest in the supremely necessary and solely sufficient word of the Word Made Flesh has not received the attention it deserves. It will show that Jesus is Mouth, Voice, Messenger, and Message. He is what God says whenever God speaks.[8] It will show that *who Jesus is* in the Prologue is precisely *what Jesus does* in the rest of the Gospel.[9] For Jesus is "'the Word' of the Father eternally spoken as his Speech, and through the sending of the Word in the flesh that Speech is spoken to [*all*] the world."[10] In all that he therefore is and says and otherwise does, ὁ λόγος is what the God and Father our Lord Jesus Christ deigns to say

---

6. Oscar Cullman, *The Christology of the New Testament,* trans. Shirley C. Guthrie and Charles A. M. Hall, rev. ed. (Philadelphia: Westminster, 1963), 259. See further "revelation and knowledge of God as the central question in Johannine theology" in Craig R. Koester, *Symbolism in the Fourth Gospel: Meaning, Mystery, Community,* 2nd ed. (Minneapolis: Fortress, 2003), 1n1.

7. To hear his word "is to receive the light of life" (Weinrich, *John 1:1–7:1,* 186). Craig R. Koester adds, "Without communication, God remains unknown and unknowable" (*The Word of Life: A Theology of John's Gospel* [Grand Rapids: Eerdmans, 2008], 25–26).

8. Weinrich, *John 1:1–7:1,* 134. In the same vein, see Andreas Köstenberger, *John,* BECNT (Grand Rapids: Baker Academic, 2004), 25. See also Koester, *Word of Life,* 25–30; and Deborah Forger, "Jesus as God's Word(s): Aurality, Epistemology, and Embodiment in the Gospel of John," *JSNT* 42 (2020): 277. Forger writes, "Only he enables others to hear God's voice."

9. "God speaks through the words Jesus utters, the actions he performs, and the death that he dies" (Koester, *Word of Life,* 27).

10. Weinrich, *John 1:1–7:1,* 135.

to a sin-sick, snake-bit world.[11] To be sure, ὁ λόγος is what the creation needs desperately to hear.

---

11. Thus, Weinrich, *John 1:1–7:1*, 191, adds, "the Word was the truly appropriate title for him of whom the Gospel speaks. For he was and remains the revelation in human form of that Speech of God which is God and which at the beginning spoke into existence a living man so that man might live with God." By his very speaking, the Speech of the God who speaks deigns again for his own to live with him.

CHAPTER ONE

THE PROLOGUE

John 1:1–18

To hear from a Sent One is to hear from his Sender. For the mouth and the voice of the one is the mouth and the voice of the other. Therefore, "from the intimacy of God a word will be spoken. A word exists to say something, and thus revelation, one of the dominating themes of the Gospel, appears in [its very] first verse."[1] God speaks when he who is God's Word comes from him whose Word the Word is. He speaks a word that must be heard if any are ever to see.

Who Jesus is in the Prologue's very first verse is a first indication of what he will do. It indicates, too, the critical importance that his word will have. It signals the foundational role that his word has always had. In the beginning (1:1), the God who created the heavens and the earth was ὁ λόγος. By his speaking this world was made (1:3). So he alone as this alone will be he who comes and the means by which he comes to reclaim and restore. By his word this world was made. By his word will it be remade. By it is there life and light (1:4). Light will shine in the darkness (1:5a). But light and darkness are diametrically opposed. So one will wane as the other waxes. One will prevail. The other will not. The capacity of the

---

1. Francis J. Moloney, *John*, SP 4 (Collegeville, MN: Liturgical Press, 1998), 35. In the same vein, see "the revelation of Jesus Christ, which God gave to [Jesus] to disclose to his servants" in Revelation 1:1; and "that which was from the beginning … concerning the Word of Life … which we proclaim also to you" in 1 John 1:1–3.

Light exceeds in every way the capacity of the darkness. In no way, then, will the darkness be able to reckon with the coming of the Light (1:5b).[2] The first creaturely witness to the coming of the Light was John (1:6). John's only purpose, his only aim, was to give witness to an even greater witness.[3] As lesser light (5:35), as "first *Christian* confessor,"[4] John shed light on the *true* Light. He marked Jesus's coming so all might believe[5] through the later one's word.[6] For the later is preeminently greater. His is a word that must be heard.[7] So the lesser gave way to the greater. One waned as the other waxed (3:30). For the lesser one's only purpose was to witness. His only objective was Israel's hearing of her Bridegroom's voice (3:29).[8] Only then will anyone hear what must be heard. Only then will anyone see.

The very character of the darkness is, however, to resist and refuse the Light.[9] So the witness of the lesser one in anticipation of the greater one was rejected. The greater one is alone the true Light (1:9). He comes to bring light to a benighted world.[10] He came to this world of his own

---

2. See further "and the darkness has not overcome/comprehended [κατέλαβεν] it" (1:5) in Andreas Köstenberger, *John*, BECNT (Grand Rapids: Baker Academic, 2004), 31n37.

3. See Jesus who is πρῶτος in 1:15, 30. See also Rev 1:17; 2:8; 22:13. When John is mentioned last, others will therefore say that "everything that John said about this [Jesus] was true" (10:41).

4. William C. Weinrich, *John 1:1–7:1*, ConcC (St. Louis: Concordia, 2015), 153 (emphasis original).

5. The verb πιστεύω, appearing here in 1:7 for the first time, occurs elsewhere in John's Gospel 98 times, almost three times as often as in Matthew, Mark, and Luke *combined*. The noun πίστις does not appear. The adjectives ἄπιστος and πιστός appear only in 20:27.

6. The apparent ambiguity of δι' αὐτοῦ (through him) at the conclusion of 1:7 is only that, apparent. The far demonstrative ἐκεῖνος (that one [was not the Light]) that follows at the beginning of 1:8 refers not to the prior and syntactically near αὐτοῦ (him) but to the prior and syntactically far understood subject of ἦλθεν and μαρτυρήσῃ in 1:7, which is the "man sent from God, whose name was John" in 1:6. Thus, δι' αὐτοῦ (through him) at the end of 1:7 means "through the Light." See the similar customary grammatical use of the near demonstrative οὗτος (this one) in 1:2, 7; the use of the far demonstrative in 1:8, 18; and the consistent referent of "through him" in 1:3, 7, 10. See also the three uses of ἵνα to introduce a purpose clause in 1:7–8 and the three uses of ὅτι to introduce a causal clause in 1:15, 16, 17. See further "through Jesus Christ" in 1:17.

7. "It is through listening" that others "ultimately come to believe," observes Deborah Forger, "Jesus as God's Word(s): Aurality, Epistemology, and Embodiment in the Gospel of John," *JSNT* 42 (2020): 277.

8. See further John as "friend of the Bridegroom" in Mary L. Coloe, "The Woman of Samaria: Her Characterization, Narrative, and Theological Significance," in *Characters and Characterization in the Gospel of John*, ed. Christopher Skinner, LNTS 461 (London: Bloomsbury, 2012), 184–88.

9. Weinrich, *John 1:1–7:1*, 150.

10. Appearing for the first time in 1:9, the noun κόσμος appears 78 times in John's Gospel. The same noun appears 8 times in Matthew, and only 3 times each in Mark and Luke.

creating. But, paradoxically, the creation did not recognize its Creator (1:10). For the darkness owns it. It is estranged and opposed. It is deaf, dumb, and blind. It is dead in the rebellion of sin. The true Light came to what was his own (1:1), to its persons and things (τὰ ἴδια). It was his prized possession. He had selected it so that it might be the instrument of his preeminent purpose. But the persons of his very own household (οἱ ἴδιοι), his very own Israel, did not receive him.[11] Instead, like the rest of the world, Israel too was inexplicably blind to him. Owned too by the darkness, it did not comprehend him. It did not receive him.[12] Like the rest of the world, it saw him but ultimately did not see him.[13]

It failed to see him because it was not able, it was not willing, to hear (8:37, 43; 14:24). But some did. Those who heard believed. Those who believed were granted an exceptional privilege. They were gifted with the extraordinary prerogative of a wholly undeserved claim to an incomparable status and authority (ἐξουσία, 1:12). Believing in his name (cf. 20:31),[14] they became his siblings (20:17; cf. 8:35). They became children of him whose Word the Word is (1:12). This did not happen by a prescribed or presumed bloodline (ἐξ αἱμάτων). Not by any suggestion of a willful capacity inherent in human flesh (ἐκ θελήματος σαρκός)[15] was it so. Neither was it achieved by the desiring or the actions of any mere man (ἐκ θελήματος ἀνδρός). Instead, by God (ἐκ θεοῦ) alone is such a thing possible (1:13). By the Spirit working through the word of the Word Made Flesh does God alone beget those he deigns to have as his own (3:3, 5).

So the Word became a fully human person (σάρξ, 1:14).[16] As in the wilderness—this time in his very own flesh—he came again to dwell with

---

11. For the play on words in 1:11, see further Köstenberger, *John*, 36–37.

12. For the Gospel's motif of their misunderstanding, see R. Alan Culpepper, *Anatomy of the Fourth Gospel: A Study in Literary Design* (Philadelphia: Fortress, 1983), 152–65.

13. Craig R. Koester observes, "God is 'from above,' and people are 'from below.' " Therefore, "to ordinary human eyes God's presence is veiled, his activity elusive." He is veiled in flesh. They must see the veiled Godhead. Thus, the world sees but does not see, for "Jesus' divine origin was hidden from human eyes; it could not be discerned 'by appearances' (7:24)," *Symbolism in the Fourth Gospel: Meaning, Mystery, Community*, 2nd ed. (Minneapolis: Fortress, 2003), 1.

14. Only John speaks of believing in the name of Jesus. See 2:23; 3:18; 1 John 3:23; 5:13.

15. The human person is completely and entirely incapable as regards such a thing.

16. See further Köstenberger, *John*, 40.

his own.[17] The dwelling place of the Lord whose glory is that of the One and Only One (μονογενής) from the Father came. And he was seen "full of grace and truth" (πλήρης χάριτος καὶ ἀληθείας, 1:14).[18] By his word this world was made. By his revelatory glory he chose for himself a house with which to dwell (14:2–3). By means of the ultimate and abiding reality, the truth, that he alone defines and is, he said what had to be spoken. He spoke so he might be seen as he must forever be seen. For to see is to be as is he (1 John 3:2).[19] So the Word Made Flesh came so all the world might see him in its hearing of him and live (5:25).

The one named John spoke of him and gave witness to him. And he gave way because he who was later was preeminently greater (πρῶτος, 1:15).[20] Out of the fullness (ἐκ τοῦ πληρώματος) of Jesus comes an infinitely greater grace. Out of Jesus comes a final, fulfilling, and completing grace. Through him is that grace to which every previous grace was intended to point.[21] Through him there is "grace for grace" (χάριν ἀντὶ χάριτος, 1:16).[22] For the prior, anticipatory grace of the promise of the Christ was given through the law (ὁ νόμος) of Moses (cf. "for he wrote of me," 5:46). But the much-anticipated final grace (χάρις) and truth (ἀλήθεια) of God became a reality through Jesus (1:17; cf. 17:3; 20:31). The prior gave way to the later and the greater. Its purpose served, it came to its end. It came to an end in favor of the enduring supremacy of what always was its end. It saw its end. For there is no longer a need for the offering of the promise when the promise has been kept.[23] As is only right, now the

---

17. For the likely meaning of ἐσκήνωσεν ("tented," "tabernacled") in 1:14 (see elsewhere in the NT the use of the verb only in Rev 7:15; 12:12; 13:6; 21:3), see further Köstenberger, *John*, 41.

18. See further Köstenberger, *John*, 44–45.

19. See "children" in 1:12. See also "son" in 8:35; and "brothers" in 20:17. See further Bruce G. Schuchard, *1–3 John*, ConcC (Saint Louis: Concordia, 2012), 319–24; and Weinrich, *John 1:1–7:1*, 158n339.

20. "The Baptist, presumably unaware of Jesus' preexistence as the Word, may simply have intended (in 1:15) to affirm that Jesus 'surpassed him.' If so, he spoke better than he knew" (Köstenberger, *John*, 45). See Colin G. Kruse, *The Gospel according to John*, TNTC (Leicester, UK: Inter-Varsity, 2003), 72.

21. "One grace after another grace," observes Marianne Meye Thompson, "taking the place of grace." *John: A Commentary*, NTL (Louisville: Westminster John Knox, 2015), 27.

22. See Köstenberger, *John*, 46–47, citing the earlier opinion of Adolf Schlatter, *Der Evangelist Johannes*, 2nd ed. (Stuttgart: Calwer, 1948), 32.

23. For Jesus as the fulfillment and replacement of Moses and the law, see Köstenberger, *John*, 46–48. See further Bruce G. Schuchard, "Temple, Festivals, and Scripture in the Gospel of John,"

focus, now all that remains, is the promise kept. Thus, the remembrance of the promise previously given serves now only to affirm and inform. It affirms and informs the present and enduring reality of the keeping of the same in the grace and truth of him who is the Truth.

No one has ever seen the God whose truth the Word Made Flesh is (1:18a; cf. 5:37; 6:46; 1 John 4:12, 20). And no one means without exception, ever.[24] For the Father who is spirit (4:24) and so is unseen is also unseen because he does not characteristically speak or act for himself. Instead, "the Word of God, spoken in eternity and from all eternity," is characteristically he alone who is "heard by man, seen by man, believed by man, followed by man, experienced by man."[25] God has a preferred and exclusive agent. He has a preferred and exclusive Spokesman, a singular way of speaking outside of himself.[26] He does not then ordinarily otherwise speak.[27] The task of "the perfect and complete revelation of God"[28] is that of the Speech of the God who speaks.[29] This task the Word Made Flesh shares with the equally unseen Spirit (3:8) that the Anointed One, the Messiah (1:41), bears. The two are inseparable (1:32–33).[30] When one is present, so is the other. When the One and Only One (1:14, 18a) speaks, they both speak.

---

in *The Oxford Handbook of Johannine Studies*, ed. Judith M. Lieu and Martinus C. de Boer (Oxford: Oxford University Press, 2018), 381–95.

24. See Koester, *Symbolism*, 1. See also Schuchard, *1–3 John*, 476–77.

25. Weinrich, *John 1:1–7:1*, 127.

26. "Jesus' words," observes Forger, "render God's thoughts audible." He is "the unique mouthpiece of God" and "the unique means by which the Father's voice can be heard" ("Jesus as God's Word(s)," 281).

27. See the shapeless and formless one who sits on the throne in Revelation 4:2–3 who does not otherwise speak. Cf. "his voice you have never heard, his form you have never seen" in John 5:34.

28. Weinrich, *John 1:1–7:1*, 134.

29. In 1:18b, then, Weinrich notes, "we find the claim of an eternal relationship between the only Son and the Father, and this claim is made for the purpose of identifying the one who gives the true revelation of God. The reality of God as the speaking God (a speaking and a being spoken) is the divine source and origin (ἀρχή, in Jn 1:1–2) out of which the Word comes and which he reveals in his words and works. The Word speaks as the Father speaks, for as Word he is the Speech of the Father." *John 1:1–7:1*, 135.

30. See further Leopoldo A. Sánchez M., *Receiver, Bearer, and Giver of God's Spirit: Jesus' Life in the Spirit as a Lens for Theology and Life* (Eugene, OR: Pickwick, 2015).

The One and Only One (μονογενής),[31] who is himself God (θεός),[32] who is himself also the One Who Is (ὁ ὤν),[33] is who Jesus is. He comes from yet never is entirely away from "the bosom of the Father" (εἰς τὸν κόλπον τοῦ πατρός; cf. 1:1).[34] He comes so that he alone might make the truth of him whose Truth the Word is known (1:18b; cf. 14:6).[35] Through the Word Made Flesh and through his word and Spirit alone are God's word and will known.[36] Through Christ alone is light given. Through Christ alone does the reality of a final, fulfilling, and completing grace come. Those without sight see (9:39). But the seeing of God as he must be seen can only be done by the one who sees Jesus as he must be seen (14:9). And the seeing of Jesus as he must be seen can only be done by the Spirit (3:3, 5), by one who takes him at his word (14:15–17, 25–26; 15:26; 16:7–8, 12–14;

---

31. For the meaning in 1:14 and 18 of μονογενής (not "only begotten" but "one and only"), see Weinrich, *John 1:1–7:1*, 110–11; and Schuchard, *1–3 John*, 439. See also Köstenberger, who offers the important observation that in Genesis 22:2, 12, 16, Isaac is Abraham's "one and only" (Heb 11:17), "even though the patriarch earlier had fathered Ishmael" and that it is Abraham's sacrifice of Isaac that likely informs the interest of Jesus in describing himself as a "one and only Son" in John 3:16 (see also 3:18; 1 John 4:9) (*John*, 42–43).

32. For the text and the syntax in 1:18 of μονογενὴς θεός, see Weinrich, *John 1:1–7:1*, 119–20.

33. Cf. the response to Moses of God in LXX Exodus 3:14, who says, ἐγώ εἰμι ὁ ὤν (I am the One Who Is). Therefore, Yahweh (see MT Exod 3:15 and the 20 times that the name Yahweh appears in MT Genesis 2–3; cf. "all things came into being through him" in John 1:3) instructs Moses to return to Israel, saying, ὁ ὢν ἀπέσταλκέν με πρὸς ὑμᾶς (The One Who Is has sent me to you). Likewise, Thompson observes, "Alluding to the LXX, the first-century Jewish exegete Philo repeatedly refers to God either as *ho ōn* ('the one who is') or, more frequently, as *to ōn*, 'that which is'" (*John*, 158). See *Somn.* 1.230–33; *Mut.* 11–15; *Deus* 62; *Det.* 160; *Decal.* 58. See further ὁ ὢν καὶ ὁ ἦν καὶ ὁ ἐρχόμενος ("the One Who Is and Who Was and Who Is To Come," Rev 1:4, 8). See also variations of the same in Revelation 4:8; 11:17; 16:5. Thus, Irenaeus maintains that the God who spoke with Moses and the rest of the prophets was the Word of God, through whom God alone speaks. They all saw the Father in their seeing of the Son (*Adv. haer.* 4.5.1 [ANF 1:466]). "For the Father is the invisible of the Son, but the Son the visible of the Father" (4.6.6 [ANF 1:469]). Cf. "He is the image of the invisible God" in Col 1:15. Apart from the Word, concurs Weinrich, "God has nothing to say" (*John 1:1–7:1*, 701–2).

34. Cf. the bosom of Abraham in Luke 16:22. For God the Father in the Gospel of John, see especially Marianne Meye Thompson, *The God of the Gospel of John* (Grand Rapids: Eerdmans, 2001).

35. See further the meaning of ἐξηγήσατο (has made [him] known) in 1:18b in Weinrich, *John 1:1–7:1*, 123–24.

36. "To hear the words of Jesus is to know those of the Father" (Forger, "Jesus as God's Word(s)," 282). For Jesus is "the exclusive means by which persons come to know the Father" (282–83). See further Luther, who states that from "the days of Adam, Christ has always revealed God to mankind" (*LW* 22:157). For the end to end double *inclusio* that frames first the Gospel's prologue (see the references to God the Father and God the Son in 1:1 and 1:18) and then frames the beginning and the end of the narrative that follows (see the references to the seeing of God in 1:18 and 20:28–29), and for Jesus as he alone who makes God known, see also Kevin L. Armbrust, "'No One Has Ever Seen God' (John 1:18): Not Seeing Yet Believing in the Gospel of John" (PhD diss., Concordia Seminary, 2014). See further discussion to come on the analysis of 20:28–29.

cf. 2:22). By word alone of the Word Made Flesh does one see what flesh and blood can in no way see. Yet such things must still be seen if any are to see God (12:45; 14:9; 20:28) and live (5:25). Therefore, never does the mere seeing of Jesus with nothing more than the naked eye suffice to inform. Many saw him yet ultimately did not see him.[37] With what follows we shall see that the completing testimony of the Word Made Flesh solely suffices to inform such seeing. Never can the sightless otherwise see.[38] *What cannot be seen must be heard*, and so God sends his Word.[39]

---

37. Such seeing "obviously cannot indicate only a physical seeing, for others also saw ... and yet they did not 'see'" (Jn 9:39; 12:40)" (Weinrich, *John 1:1–7:1*, 109).

38. Cf. the purpose of Paul's witness, which is "to open their eyes" in Acts 26:18. See also "salve to anoint your eyes" in Revelation 3:18; and "enlightened eyes of the heart" in Ephesians 1:18.

39. Cf. the need not just to see but also to hear in 1 John 1:1, 3 (see also Matt 13:16; Mark 8:18; Luke 24:30–32); and the purpose of Torah to "enlighten the eyes" in Psalm 19:8.

CHAPTER TWO

A FIRST JOURNEY *to* JERUSALEM *in* ANTICIPATION *of the* COMING *of* HIS HOUR

John 1:19–3:36

In the story of Jesus that follows (1:19–3:36), Jesus goes to Jerusalem the first of the three times that he will do this in the first half of the Gospel (1:19–10:42).[1] When he does this a fourth and final time, in the Gospel's second half (11:1–20:31), the time for his hour will come (12:23, 27; 13:1; 16:25, 32; 17:1; 19:14).[2] A second significant figure marks these days. Conspicuously, the days begin and end not with Jesus but with John (see 1:19–28, 29–34, 35–37; 3:25–30).[3] They *emblematically* begin when John *sees but does not see* (1:31, 33). For his speaking depends on the speaking

---

1. See below the second and third occasions in which Jesus makes his way to the Holy City in 4:1–5:47 and in 6:1–10:42.

2. For Jesus as pilgrim Messiah in the first half of the Gospel (1:19–10:42) in anticipation of the arrival and accomplishment of the hour of Jesus in the Gospel's second half (11:1–20:31), and for the Gospel's consistent use of *inclusios* to mark such structures, see Bruce G. Schuchard, "The Wedding Feast at Cana and the Christological Monomania of St. John," in *All Theology is Christology: Essays in Honor of David P. Scaer*, ed. Dean O. Wenthe et al. (Fort Wayne, IN: Concordia Theological Seminary Press, 2000), 101–16. See further Bruce G. Schuchard, "Form versus Function: Citation Technique and Authorial Intention in the Gospel of John," in *Abiding Words: The Use of Scripture in the Gospel of John*, ed. Alicia D. Myers and Bruce G. Schuchard, RBS 81 (Atlanta: SBL Press, 2015), 35–45. See also those surveyed by Johannes Beutler, *A Commentary on the Gospel of John*, trans. Michael Tait (Grand Rapids: Eerdmans, 2017), 4–8.

3. See Schuchard, "Form versus Function," 36–37. For the *inclusio* that encompasses 1:19–3:36, see also Andreas Köstenberger, *John*, BECNT (Grand Rapids: Baker Academic, 2004), 133n1.

of the one who sent John to be a witness. Only with the aid of the voice from heaven (1:33) does John see. He sees the one whose voice is to be heard above all other voices.[4] Only then does John help others to see what he has seen. First John hears. Then he sees and believes. He testifies. And then he defers to the preeminent speaking of Jesus.[5]

"I did not know him," declares John, not once but twice (1:31, 33). John did not initially know that his own relative (Luke 1:36) was Messiah.[6] "But the one who sent me to baptize with water," adds John, "that one said to me, 'Upon whomever you see the Spirit descending and remaining, this is he who baptizes with the Holy Spirit' " (1:33).[7] Therefore, only when the voice from heaven informs what John is seeing (1:32) does John *see one thing*, see Jesus, *and believe another.*[8] Only then does John see that Jesus is "the Lamb of God who takes away the sin of the world" (1:29).[9] "And I have seen," adds John, "and I have borne witness that this is the Son of God" (1:34; cf. great David's greater Son in Ps 2:7).[10] From an unnamed witness in heaven above (1:33) to another witness on earth below with

---

4. See also the telling pronouncement of the Father in each of the Synoptic Gospels at the transfiguration of Jesus, where the Father says, "Listen to him" (Matt 17:5; Mark 9:7; Luke 9:35). Elsewhere, such extraordinarily rare cases of the Father speaking for himself conspicuously seem to serve in similar terms to direct all attention to Jesus as he who must be heard. See, e.g., John 12:27–28.

5. See the waning of John and his testimony in the narration of the Gospel's first three days (1:19–28, 29–34, 35–42), which overlaps with the waxing of Jesus and his testimony in his first three days (1:29–34, 35–42, 43–51), culminating in the first of the seven signs of Jesus, in 2:1–11. See further John's three answers to three questions (1:20–21), his threefold use of the near demonstrative (οὗτος) to confess further the significance of Jesus (1:30, 33, 34), and his overall significance in the first half of the Gospel in Catrin H. Williams, "John (the Baptist): The Witness on the Threshold," in *Character Studies in the Fourth Gospel: Narrative Approaches to Seventy Figures in John*, ed. Steven A. Hunt et al. (Grand Rapids: Eerdmans, 2013), 45–60. Cf. the explicit statement of John in 3:30: "That one must increase, but I must decrease." At the conclusion of John 3, John speaks for the last time (3:25–30; see also 4:1). He is not, however, forgotten. See the recurring prominence of John at the conclusion of John 5 (5:33–36) and John 10 (10:40–42).

6. In the course of what follows it will be increasingly apparent that there is even more than this that John does not know about Jesus.

7. See further the Gospel's interest in water in Craig R. Koester, *Symbolism in the Fourth Gospel: Meaning, Mystery, Community*, 2nd ed. (Minneapolis: Fortress, 2003), 175–206.

8. Thus, John denies knowing Jesus "because in this Gospel knowledge of Jesus, that is, who he really is in relation to the Father, can only come by revelation," notes D. Moody Smith, *John*, ANTC (Nashville: Abingdon, 1999), 70.

9. That the Gospel's Lamb is to be interpreted as an amalgam of three backgrounds—the Passover lamb, Isaac, and Isaiah's suffering servant—is argued persuasively by William C. Weinrich, *John 1:1–7:1*, ConcC (St. Louis: Concordia, 2015), 237–49. See further Richard Bauckham, *Gospel of Glory: Major Themes in Johannine Theology* (Grand Rapids: Baker Academic, 2015), 154–59.

10. See the force of this early reference to Jesus as Son of God in the analysis of 1:51.

reference to a third preeminent witness, each initial witness points to the other. Each points to the witness whose speaking must finally inform. Each heralds the solely sufficient revelation of God whose truth the Word Made Flesh is.

As "the *voice* of one crying in the wilderness" (1:23),[11] John confesses further, saying, "I baptize with water, but among you stands one whom you do not know, even he who comes after me, the strap of whose sandal I am not worthy to untie" (1:26–27).[12] Thus, John's baptism with water makes straight the way (1:23) for the greater baptism of Jesus, which will be with the Holy Spirit (1:33). A preliminary grace heralds the coming of a surpassingly greater grace (cf. 1:16), "the reality to which John with his water baptism only pointed."[13] Earthly water anticipates a begetting from above (3:3) by God (1:13) by means of heavenly water, which is the Spirit of Truth (3:5). The eschatological cleansing of the age that is to come is nigh.

By the salvific flood of the earthly blood and heavenly water of the Word Made Flesh (19:34) will a final cleansing come.[14] By a later and greater Passover[15] will a later grace fulfill and so take the place of every previous grace. John heralds the imminence of these things. Through the greater baptism of Jesus that is of the Holy Spirit will they finally come. Jesus will preeminently reveal, for he alone bears and confers in full measure the eschatological Spirit.[16] But the Spirit comes only to those who hear Jesus's word. By the Spirit through the word of the Word Made Flesh

---

11. For the citation in 1:23, the figure of John, and for all other explicit citations of the Old Testament in the Gospel of John, see Bruce G. Schuchard, *Scripture within Scripture: The Interrelationship of Form and Function in the Explicit Old Testament Citations in the Gospel of John*, SBLDS 133 (Atlanta: Scholars Press, 1992). See further Schuchard, "Form versus Function," 23–45.

12. For the taking off of a master's shoe as the work of a slave, see Köstenberger, *John*, 65. Thus, John proclaims that he is not even worthy of being Jesus's slave.

13. Herman Ridderbos, *The Gospel of John: A Theological Commentary*, trans. John Vriend (Grand Rapids: Eerdmans, 1997), 77. See also Ardel Caneday, "The Word Made Flesh as Mystery Incarnate: Revealing and Concealing Dramatized by Jesus as Portrayed in John's Gospel," *JETS* 60 (2017): 761.

14. See further analysis of 19:34.

15. In the Gospel's first half (1:19–10:42), a first Passover (2:13) and a second (6:4) anticipate the summing importance of the Gospel's third and final Passover, which is first mentioned in the Gospel's second half (11:1–20:31) as early as 11:55 and from that juncture forward continues as a dominant element that defines what follows.

16. Cf. the expectation of an eschatological outpouring of the Holy Spirit in Isaiah 32:15; 44:3; Ezekiel 36:25–27; Joel 2:28–32.

is the God that no one has ever seen (1:18) known. Not only is the word of Jesus necessary. The word of Jesus is *solely sufficient*. Only his word informs in necessarily final terms who Jesus is. Only his word informs the purpose to the dying and the rising of the Word Made Flesh.

Many hear and believe and follow. Two who do so are John's own disciples. The first is Andrew and the other is *never named* (1:35–39).[17] Andrew recruits his brother (Simon Peter) (1:40–42). Jesus calls Philip (1:43–44). Philip summons Nathanael (1:45–51). Each hears from another. Only on the basis of what they hear do Jesus's five first disciples come. When others do so they too will see what it means for Jesus to be the herald of him whose Word the Word is. For this reason, the very first words in the Gospel of John that the Word Made Flesh speaks are a conspicuously couched question.[18] Jesus sees that the disciples of John are following Jesus in response to what they have heard from John. So he asks them, "What do you seek?" (1:38).[19] He does not wait for an answer. "Come and you will see" (1:39), adds Jesus (cf. 1:46). For greater things than what they have seen so far must they ultimately see (1:50). Greater things will they see when the Teacher (1:38) teaches what only he can teach. Only then will they see that the "Teacher and the content of his teaching are one and the same."[20] Thus, the words "What do you seek?" and "Come and you will see" invite those who hear them to a full-scale consideration of Jesus. They beckon to a fundamentally new way of hearing both Moses and the prophets (1:45). They summon to what can only happen through the word of the Word

---

17. That he is never named, observes Köstenberger (citing others), "can best be explained if the disciple was John the evangelist, since he never refers to himself by name in this Gospel" (*John*, 76). Not only is he not named. The Gospel does not refer to him again until the night of Jesus's betrayal. See further the importance of the Evangelist as a figure in his own Gospel from beginning to end in Bauckham, *Gospel of Glory*, 150–53.

18. For the rhetorical significance of the questions of Jesus in John, see Douglas Estes, *The Questions of Jesus in John: Logic, Rhetoric, and Persuasive Discourse*, BibInt 115 (Leiden: Brill, 2013).

19. Here, the first of Jesus's questions challenges also the hearer of the Gospel to ask what it is that the hearer seeks. See D. A. Carson, *The Gospel according to John*, PNTC (Grand Rapids: Eerdmans, 1991), 154–55. See also Bauckham, *Gospel of Glory*, 151–53, who also persuasively argues that the anonymous disciple with Andrew in 1:35–40 must be the Beloved Disciple, who appears just before the Gospel's first reference to Peter in 1:40–42 and at the end of its last reference to Peter in 21:20–23. As ideal witness, the Beloved Disciple is thus present at the beginning and at the end.

20. Weinrich, *John 1:1–7:1*, 275.

Made Flesh.[21] Only when one comes to him, hears him, and takes him at his word is one a *true Israelite* (1:47).[22] Only then does one see.[23]

Jesus shows that he knows what no ordinary human person can possibly know[24] when he says to Nathanael, "Before Philip called you, while you were under the fig tree, I saw you" (1:48). What Jesus says causes Nathanael to see. Nathanael sees that Jesus is the promised royal Son of God (see great David's greater Son in Ps 2:7) that Israel has awaited (1:49; see also 1:34).[25] Nathanael confesses Jesus rightly. The others do so as well.[26] But the disciples of Jesus also show that what they thus far know has its limits. What they know is that Jesus's father is Joseph and that Jesus is from Nazareth (1:45). Bound by their earthly frame of reference (3:31; see also 3:6), there is so much more that they still must know. There are heavenly realities and purposes to Jesus that they must come to know, that they must therefore see. They will see these things when they hear

---

21. Thus, the invitation to come and see is extended also to every ancient or modern hearer of what follows. See Koester, *Word of Life*, 2.

22. See especially the defining need of Israel to hear in the Shema of LXX Deuteronomy 6:3–4 and in Mark 12:29. See further LXX Deuteronomy 4:1; 5:1; 9:1; 20:3; 27:9; Psalm 49:7; 81:8; Hosea 4:1; 5:1; Amos 3:1; Micah 3:9; Isaiah 44:1; 46:3; 48:1, 12; Jereremiah 2:4; 10:1; Ezekiel 6:3; 13:2; 18:25; 36:1, 4. For Nathanael as a corresponding "symbol of Israel coming to God," see Raymond Brown, *The Gospel according to John I–XII*, AB 29A (Garden City, NY: Doubleday, 1966), 82.

23. "It may be that the evangelist is playing on the common notion that the name Israel means 'seeing God' and that this suggested the reference to Jacob's vision in Jn 1:51" (Weinrich, *John 1:1–7:1*, 289). See Philo, *Fug.* 208.

24. See further the analysis of 2:24–25.

25. For the expectation that sitting under a fig tree would be the experience of the end-time people of God (1 Kgs 4:25; Isa 36:16; Mic 4:4; Zech 3:10) and the suggestion that Jesus's words would have prompted an association with the messianic Branch of Zechariah 3:8 (see also Gen 49:10; Num 24:17; Zech 6:12; Jer 23:5; 33:15; cf. Isa 11:1), a figure that first-century Jews would have seen as Son of God (meaning royal Son of David of Ps 2) and king of Israel (1:49), see Köstenberger, *John*, 83. See also Bauckham, *Gospel of Glory*, 166–71. That "Nazareth" (1:45–46) and "Nazarene" (18:5, 7; 19:19) would have also prompted similar associations is suggested by Mary L. Coloe, "The Nazarene King: Pilate's Title as the Key to John's Crucifixion," in *The Death of Jesus in the Fourth Gospel*, ed. Gilbert Van Belle, BETL 200 (Leuven: Leuven University Press, 2007), 839–48.

26. See 1:29 ("Lamb of God who takes away the sin of the world"), 33 ("he who baptizes with the Holy Spirit"), 34 ("Son of God"), 36 ("Lamb of God"), 38 ("Rabbi"), 41 ("Messiah"; elsewhere in the NT the term appears only in 4:25), 45 ("him of whom Moses in the law and also the prophets wrote"), 49 ("Rabbi," "Son of God," "King of Israel"). To this Jesus adds "Son of Man" (1:51). See further Köstenberger, *John*, 84, who notes rightly that Nathanael's words "Rabbi, you are the Son of God! You are the King of Israel!" in 1:49 add little to what the others have already said. See also Koester, *Symbolism*, 179. With "Son of God" (cf. 1:34) and "King of Israel" Nathanael confesses that he too has come to believe that Jesus is Messiah. See 2 Samuel 7:14; Psalm 2:7; and the juxtaposition of "Son of God" and "Christ" in Luke 4:41.

more than they have thus far heard. *Hearing more, they will see more* than unaided eyes can ever see. With Spirit-wrought eyes of faith they will see an open rather than a closed heaven, and heaven and earth united as a single Bethel (1:51), a single "house of God."[27] When Jesus is risen and the Spirit is given (20:22), then will they see (2:22; see also 8:28; 12:16).[28] For unless one is born from above of heavenly water, which is the Spirit (3:3, 5), one will never see.

On a third day (2:1) after the one described in 1:43–51, at the end of an initial, conspicuously constructed, six-day-long week of days,[29] Jesus and his disciples attend with his mother a wedding feast (γάμος)[30] in Cana of Galilee (2:1). But the feast is lacking what a feast requires. The wine of the feast is in short supply (ὑστερήσαντος οἴνου, 2:3).[31] So Jesus's hopeful mother[32] instructs the servants of the feast to wait on the word of the

---

27. Therefore, long before Nathanael responds to Philip's invitation to "come and see" (1:46), long before he comes and sees, he is seen (1:50a). Only then does he see. Only then does Jesus promise that "greater things than these things will you see" (1:50b). Only then will they see (1:51).

28. See further on the analysis of 2:22.

29. "On the next day" (τῇ ἐπαύριον) in 1:29, 35, and 43 (see also 6:22; 12:12) makes plain and prominent the passing of a second, third, and fourth day in John 1. "On the third day" (τῇ ἡμέρᾳ τῇ τρίτῃ) in 2:1 specifies further that a day followed day four in 1:43–51 that was *two days later*. Cf. the death of Jesus on Good Friday followed by his Easter Sunday resurrection "on the third day" in Matthew 16:21; 17:23; 20:19; 27:64; Luke 9:22; 18:33; 24:7, 21, 46; Acts 10:40; 1 Corinthians 15:4; cf. John 2:19–21. See further the foreshadowing significance of Cana's feast on a "third day" that is also a sixth day in Schuchard, "Wedding Feast." Cf. "the six-day-long first creation whose life-creating labor accomplished by the same creator (1:3) likewise achieved its nuptial telos on day six" in Schuchard, "Form versus Function" (38n67). For the intriguing suggestion that John 2:1 also recalls Exodus 19 at the time of "the third new moon after the people of Israel had gone out of the land of Egypt" (19:1) when at Sinai "on the third day" (19:11, 15, 16) God descended from above to reveal himself to Israel (see esp. "in the sight of all the people," 19:11) and to make her his own (see "I bore you on eagles' wings and brought you to myself" and "you shall be my treasured possession among all the peoples," 19:4–5), see Francis J. Moloney, *John*, SP 4 (Collegeville, MN: Liturgical Press, 1998), 66. See further Mary L. Coloe, "The Johannine Pentecost: John 1:19–2.12," *AusBR* 35 (2007): 41–56; and Coloe, "The Servants/Steward at Cana: The 'Whispering Wizards'' Wine Bearers," in Hunt et al., *Character Studies in the Fourth Gospel*, 228–32.

30. See the use of γάμος in Matthew 22:2–12; 25:10; Luke 12:36; 14:8; Hebrews 13:4; Revelation 19:7, 9.

31. Cf. Israel, which lacks what would make it complete.

32. See elsewhere his mother only in 19:25–27. See further on her significance in the analysis of 19:25–27.

Word Made Flesh.[33] "Do whatever he says to you" (2:5), says his mother.[34] Six water jars of stone[35] are present so that, at the feast, everyone and everything might be ritually clean in keeping with the law of Moses (2:6).[36] Ritual cleansing anticipates a greater cleansing that will come with the age that is to come. The Word Made Flesh speaks. And the jars are filled to the top with water (2:7). He speaks again. And water becomes wine.[37] For water and wine will both flow from his riven side (19:34).[38] *A bath becomes a beverage.* For a final bath and a final beverage, a baptismal flood of the Spirit and a paschal feast of victory, will both come when the Bridegroom (3:29) sheds his blood.[39] As is only right, the best will be saved for last (2:10).[40] It will cleanse (13:3–11). It will slake. And those who thirst will thirst no more (4:13; 6:55).[41] Therefore, at Cana, the beginning (ἀρχή) of

---

33. For "man does not live by bread alone, but *man lives by every word that comes from the mouth of God*" (Deut 8:3). Therefore, Martin Luther suggests that "these servants are all preachers of the New Testament like the apostles and their successors," *Sermons of Martin Luther*, vol. 1, *Sermons on Gospel Texts for Advent, Christmas, and Epiphany*, ed. John Nicholas Lenker, trans. John Nicholas Lenker et al. (repr., Grand Rapids: Baker, 1989), 68. Originally published as *The Precious and Sacred Writings of Martin Luther*, vol 10, *Luther's Church Postil: Gospels: Advent, Christmas, and Epiphany* (Minneapolis: Lutherans in All Lands, 1905). See also Augustine, *Homilies* 9.5.

34. Cf. the words of Pharaoh to all of Egypt with reference to Joseph in LXX Gen 41:55. See further Schuchard, "Wedding Feast," 115n61.

35. Stone was characteristically resistant to contamination. See Köstenberger, *John*, 96.

36. They were there κατὰ τὸν καθαρισμὸν τῶν Ἰουδαίων ("for the [ritual] purification of the Jews").

37. Cf. the expectation of a similar provision in Genesis 49:10–11; Isaiah 25:6; Jeremiah 31:12–14; Hosea 14:7; Amos 9:13–14; Joel 3:18; 2 Baruch 29:5; 1 Enoch 10:19. See also Matthew 22:1–14; 25:1–13.

38. See further Schuchard, "Wedding Feast," 115n63. Therefore, what Jesus gives at Cana is neither the heavenly reality that later he will ultimately provide nor is it the earthly reality that was the concern of his mother, for which she approached him. What he gives exceeds her expectation in every way and thus anticipates his.

39. Cf. Moses, the "bridegroom of blood," also by virtue of the rending of flesh and the spilling of blood (through circumcision) in Exodus 4:24–26. At Cana, "Jesus takes up the idea that the messianic ruler will cleanse with wine [see Gen 49:10–11] by transforming the water that was ordinarily used for cleansing into fine wine. Again, the biblical prophets promised that when God restored Davidic rule, he would pour out his favor on Israel, so that 'the mountains will drip sweet wine, and all the hills shall flow with it' (Amos 9:13; cf. Joel 3:18; Isa 25:6). Jesus's actions fit this promise, since the quantity of wine he produced was enormous," notes Craig R. Koester, *The Word of Life: A Theology of John's Gospel* (Grand Rapids: Eerdmans, 2008), 92–93.

40. Cf. in LXX Psalm 23:5 the cup of the Lord who is Shepherd that "inebriates/makes happy [μεθύσκον] like the very best [wine]." Contrast in 2:11 the steward who posits that ordinarily the good wine is served first, and "when [the guests] are inebriated [μεθυσθῶσιν], the lesser, but you have kept the good wine until now"; and Luther, who posits that the steward who knows nothing regarding the source of the wine "is the old priesthood among the Jews who knew naught but works" (*Sermons*, 69). See further the steward in Sirach 32:1–2.

41. Contrast Jesus who declares, "I thirst," and thus thirsts for the thirsty in 19:28. See Koester, *Word of Life*, 146.

Jesus's signs (2:11), like each and every one of his signs, anticipates the end that will come[42] with the accomplishment of his hour (2:4).[43] At Cana, his Bride sees and believes (2:11).[44] And with him she remains (2:12).

The feast of the Jews, the Passover, punctuates what follows (2:13; see also 2:23). A first week (1:19–2:11) and a first trip to Jerusalem for a first Passover (see also the Passover but no trip in 6:4) all anticipate the fated final week of the Gospel's third and final Passover (12:1–19:42).[45] So, here, the Lamb of God who takes away the sin of the world (1:29, 36) goes straight to the place of the presence and the place of sacrifice that was the temple (2:14). *The* Temple (2:21; cf. 1:14), Jesus, signals with his clearing of the temple (2:15–17) the end that will come (cf. 1:16–17) when his end comes.[46] When challenged by others (2:18), he declines their demand for a self-validating sign. Instead, he speaks of what they should be seeing

---

42. The cross, observes Koester, will mark the "the culmination (*telos*) of his works" (*Symbolism*, 86; see further 82–86). Thus, it becomes "the distinctive lens through which all the [Gospel's] symbols should be viewed" (261), the "final action presaged in all of Jesus' other actions" (265). For the suggestion that the first of Jesus's signs is thus a "master sign" and "the archetype of all the signs," see Schuchard, "Wedding Feast," 114n56. Thus, Caneday observes that "Jesus completes, supersedes, and renders Jewish water purification rites, representative of the entire system of ceremonial observance, old, obsolete, and ready to pass away" ("Word Made Flesh," 757).

43. See the hour (ὥρα) of Jesus in 7:30; 8:20; 12:23, 27; 13:1; 16:32; 17:1. "In the framework of the entire Gospel," Jesus's hour "refers to the moment at which God is fully glorified in him: the hour of his death, which for Jesus constitutes also the moment of Jesus' exaltation (his 'lifting up' [3:14; 8:28; 12:32])" (Köstenberger, *John*, 95). For the foreshadowing purpose of the signs of Jesus in the Gospel of John, see the early remarks of Mathias Rissi, "Die Hochzeit in Kana (Joh 2,1–11)," in *Oikonomia: Heilsgeschichte als Thema der Theologie. Oscar Cullmann zum 65. Geburtstag*, ed. Felix Christ (Hamburg: Reich, 1967), 77. Rissi argues that the signs of Jesus in John have this consistent purpose. See further Schuchard, "Form versus Function," 37n61. See also Weinrich, *John 1:1–7:1*, 171.

44. "The presence of Jesus' mother at Cana and the cross" (see 19:25–27), observes Koester, "reinforces the idea that the glory manifested in the wine and in Jesus' death must be understood together" (*Symbolism*, 86). See further 239–42.

45. Contrast the deliberate anonymity of the festival in 5:1 in favor of the early prominence of Passover in 2:13 and 6:4. Only when the Gospel's principal interest in Passover is established do Tabernacles (7:2) and Dedication (10:22) make related contributions. The Gospel's third and final Passover is first mentioned in 11:55 and from that juncture forward remains a dominant element that defines what follows. See "six days before the Passover" (12:1); "before the feast of the Passover" (13:1); "so they might eat the Passover"(18:28); "at the Passover" (18:39); and "now it was the day of Preparation which was the Passover" (19:14).

46. See Koester, *Symbolism*, 79, 82, 86–89; and the chapter titled "Exodus 12 and the Passover Theme in John" in Stanley E. Porter, *Sacred Tradition in the New Testament: Tracing Old Testament Themes in the Gospels and Epistles* (Grand Rapids: Baker Academic, 2016), 127–51 (esp. 137–38). See further on the analysis of "he loved them to the end" in 13:1. Thus, John declares not that Jesus is a lamb of God but that he is *the* Lamb of God "par excellence" (Köstenberger, *John*, 66). For the expectation also of a new temple, see 102.

in his signs[47] that they are not. "Destroy this Temple, and in three days I will raise it up," he says (2:19). For with the coming of a third and final Passover he will do on its third day what no mere man can do. He will raise himself up (cf. 10:17–18) and will claim and impart to his Bride what he has accomplished with his sacrifice of himself. He will do what he has come to do that only he can do. On the day of the feast that defines his end, when its end is served and it sees its end, the result will be what was its end, a feast that knows no end.[48]

But when Jesus spoke of these things, *no one* perceived that he was speaking of the temple of his body (2:20–21).[49] Only when risen and the Spirit is given (20:22)[50] will any of them remember (2:22; see also 8:28; 12:16). Only then will any of them see what the Scripture (in 2:17)[51] and the Word Made Flesh (in 2:19) were saying.[52] Only then will they with new eyes see[53] what flesh-and-blood eyes can in no way see. And yet such things must still be seen if any are to see and live. "Now when he was in Jerusalem at the Passover, at the feast,[54] many believed [ἐπίστευσαν] in his name because they had seen the signs that he was doing" (2:23). They see and believe. But Jesus does not entrust (πιστεύω) himself to their initial manner of trusting in him. He does not because he sees and knows all things as regards the human person (ἄνθρωπος, 2:24–25; see further

---

47. Because Jesus is all-knowing (2:24-25), he knows that the interest of those who challenge him lacks what must in the end inform the foreshadowing purpose of his signs. See Schuchard, *Scripture within Scripture*, 27–29. See further Schuchard, "Form versus Function," 37n61. He therefore declines their interest and instead speaks of the death and resurrection that is the pronounced and consistent interest of his signs. "Verbal commentary is needed," observes Koester, because "Jesus' signs can be taken in sharply different ways" (*Word of Life*, 9). Only when words from and about Jesus inform will the purpose of his signs and that of his action in the temple be seen (164).

48. Cf. "But take heart; I have overcome the world" in 16:33. See also 1 John 2:13-14; 4:4; 5:4-5; and the prior superabundant wine of the nuptial feast at Cana given on the third day in 2:1-11. See further "those called to the supper of the marriage feast of the Lamb" in Revelation 19:9; and the bread that Jesus gives for the life of the world that is his flesh in John 6:51.

49. See elsewhere σῶμα (body) only with the death and resurrection of Jesus in 19:31, 38, 40; 20:12.

50. See further on the analysis of "born from above" and "of water and the Spirit" in 3:3, 5.

51. See further Schuchard, "Form versus Function," 30n33.

52. Richard B. Hays observes the meaning of his prophetic words "could be seen ... only after he had embodied (their) figural sense" ("Reading Scripture in Light of the Resurrection," in *The Art of Reading Scripture*, ed. Ellen F. Davis and Richard B. Hays [Grand Rapids: Eerdmans, 2003]). See further the promise that they will see in 1:51; 8:27-28, 31-32; 13:7; 14:20, 25-26; 15:26-27; 16:13-15.

53. Similarly, see Richard B. Hays, *Echoes of Scripture in the Gospels* (Waco: Baylor University Press, 2016), 311-12.

54. Thus, Passover punctuates the beginning and the end of 2:13-25.

3:1). Therefore, he knows that their believing in him lacks now what must in the end inform it.[55] He therefore knows that, when later tested, their believing in him will come to an end. Only that faith that later sees better because it hears better will finally see what they are failing to see.

An emblematic human person (ἄνθρωπος; cf. 2:25) follows (3:1). Nicodemus, a man of the Pharisees and a ruler of the Jews,[56] comes "by night" (νυκτός, 3:2). And he speaks from the less-than-informed perspective of those who have believed in Jesus on account of his signs (2:23).[57] He greets Jesus in terms of what he and those like him have thus far seen, saying, "Rabbi, we[58] know that you, a teacher, have come from God, for no one is able to do these signs that you are doing unless God is with him" (3:2). Jesus, who sees and knows all things (2:24–25), focuses first on Nicodemus' suggestion that Nicodemus knows who it is and what it is that he and the rest have been seeing. For Nicodemus has spoken a truth that is greater than he knows (3:2).[59] Jesus, who comes to give sight to the sightless (9:39), answers. He says that unless one is born "from above" (ἄνωθεν, 3:3)[60] of heavenly "water, which is the Spirit" (ὕδατος καὶ[61] πνεύματος, 3:5)[62]

---

55. Rodney A Whitacre notes that the problem is not signs-based faith per se. Instead, by definition all faith prior to the death and resurrection of Jesus and the giving of the Holy Spirit is preliminary. *John*, IVPNTC 4 (Downers Grove, IL: InterVarsity, 1999), 86. Thus, Bauckham observes that "the first disciples at first believe no more about Jesus than could easily be expected of them at this stage in the narrative." *Gospel of Glory*, 162.

56. Nicodemus is then a sitting member of the Sanhedrin (11:47). But with what follows he will also be an atypical Pharisee, an atypical ruler of the Jews. See further 7:50–52; 19:38–42.

57. See Köstenberger, *John*, 115–17, 121. For Jesus as the Gospel's "primary representative figure" and for its use of representative figures here and elsewhere, see Koester, *Symbolism*, 33–77.

58. For the use of the plural "we" when a character acts as a spokesperson for a group, see Koester, *Symbolism*, 35.

59. For the nature and function of irony in the Gospel, see R. Alan Culpepper, *Anatomy of the Fourth Gospel: A Study in Literary Design* (Philadelphia: Fortress, 1983), 165–80; Paul D. Duke, *Irony in the Fourth Gospel* (Atlanta: John Knox, 1985); Gail R. O'Day, *Revelation in the Fourth Gospel: Narrative Mode and Theological Claim* (Philadelphia: Fortress, 1986), 11–32.

60. Cf. the parallelism of 3:31, where "the one who comes from above" (ὁ ἄνωθεν ἐρχόμενος) is equated with "the one who comes from heaven" (ὁ ἐκ τοῦ οὐρανοῦ ἐρχόμενος). See also "you must be born from above" in 3:7.

61. See the explanatory use of καί in Daniel B. Wallace, *Greek Grammar beyond the Basics: An Exegetical Syntax of the New Testament* (Grand Rapids: Zondervan, 1996), 673.

62. See Charles H. Talbert, *Reading John: A Literary and Theological Commentary on the Fourth Gospel and the Johannine Epistles*, Reading the New Testament (New York: Crossroad, 1992), 99. Cf. "born of God" in 1:13; "born from above" in 3:3, 7; and "born of the Spirit" in 3:6, 8. Therefore, following Jesus's offer of "living water" in 7:38 (see also his offer of the same to the Samaritan woman in 4:10–14), 7:39 states, "Now he said this about the Spirit."

never will one see (3:3).[63] Like the Father (1:18), the Spirit too is character-istically unseen (3:8). But the voice (φωνή) of the Spirit can and must be heard (3:8)[64] in the mouth and voice of the Word Made Flesh (3:13). Where one is there is the other. The two are inseparable. Therefore, one hears the voice of the Spirit in the voice of the Word Made Flesh and sees that Jesus is the Voice of the one who sends them both, or never will one see.[65]

Sadly, Nicodemus, the teacher of Israel (3:10), resists what he hears. He does not receive (3:11),[66] and he does not believe (3:12). Others will do so as well.[67] The problem is not what the Word Made Flesh is saying, or how he chooses to say it. In this world he speaks. By means of this world's everyday earthly things (τὰ ἐπίγεια, 3:12) he naturally and nec-essarily communicates.[68] He speaks so the persons of this world may see in his earthly manner of speaking the things of heaven above.[69] But Nicodemus resists the word of the Word Made Flesh and therefore fails to see.[70] To switch to an otherworldly way of speaking will not help.[71] To communicate by means of heavenly signifiers (τὰ ἐπουράνια, 3:12) would

---

63. Neither then is he able to enter (εἰσελθεῖν) (3:5).

64. For the wordplay here involving the use of the Greek word for a "voice" or a "sound" (φωνή) and its use elsewhere in 3:29; 5:25, 28, 37; 10:3–5, 16, 27; 11:43; 12:28, 30; and 18:37, see Craig S. Keener, *The Gospel of John* (Peabody, MA: Hendrickson, 2003), 1:557–58.

65. What Jesus speaks, "that the Spirit effects" or it effects nothing (Weinrich, *John 1:1–7:1*, 450).

66. "We" in 3:11 ("*we* speak what *we* know and *we* testify to what *we* have seen, but *you* [plural] do not receive *our* testimony") unites the testimony of Jesus with that of John (cf. "I have seen and I have testified") in 1:34. That "disciples of both teachers may have been present as well" is suggested by Köstenberger, *John*, 117.

67. Therefore, Jesus responds to Nicodemus' use of "we" in 3:2 not only with a "we" of his own but also with "you" (plural) when he says, "you do not receive our testimony ... you do not believe" in 3:11–12; cf. 1:19–28; 2:18–21. Thus, in Nicodemus we see why it was that Jesus refrained from entrusting himself to the initial believing of the many in 2:23–25. We see what will soon happen when the believing of the many that lacks what must in the end inform it is challenged by the word that must inform it.

68. Cf. "He who is of the earth belongs to the earth and speaks in an earthly way" in 3:31. See also Paul's similar way of speaking of the heavenly and the earthly in 1 Corinthians 15:40; 2 Corinthians 5:1; Philemon 2:10; 3:19; and James in James 3:15.

69. Craig R. Koester notes as "God's way of communicating, the Word meets human beings in human terms" ("Jesus' Resurrection, the Signs, and the Dynamics of Faith," in *The Resurrection of Jesus in the Gospel of John*, ed. Craig R. Koester and Reimund Bieringer, WUNT 222 [Tubingen: Mohr Siebeck, 2008], 47).

70. "From start to finish, nearly everything Jesus says is misunderstood. When he speaks of heavenly things and the Spirit, his hearers think of earthly things," observes Kelli S. O'Brien, "Written That You May Believe: John 20 and Narrative Rhetoric," *CBQ* 67 (2005): 287.

71. See Koester, *Word of Life*, 28–29, 31, 37, 112.

only make matters worse. To do so would make the word of the Word Made Flesh utterly incomprehensible to earthbound ears.[72]

Just as Moses lifted up the serpent in the wilderness (Num 21:8–9), so must the Son of Man be lifted up (3:14).[73] Just as Israel looked to the uplifted serpent so must this world look to Jesus for life (3:15) and for light. "For God so loved the world that he gave his one and only Son [τὸν υἱὸν τὸν μονογενῆ],[74] that everyone who believes in him should not perish but have instead the life of the age to come" (3:16). Not to hear, not to receive and believe, is inexplicably to love the darkness and to hate the Light (3:19–20). Whether the persons of this world initially or entirely understand him or not, they must take his word to heart if any are ever to come to the Light (3:21). They must come and believe if any are ever to see.

Jesus descends from above. He bears witness to what he alone has seen and heard. "Yet no one receives his testimony" (3:32). Only the one who takes his witness to heart and believes it (1:12) confirms that God is true (3:33). Therefore, whether one initially or entirely understands or not, what one sees *and* hears one must accept. To fail to do so is to fail to see both the person and the purpose to the dying and the rising. "He whom God has sent utters the words of God" (3:34a). He whom God has sent thereby also "gives the Spirit without measure" (3:34b). Therefore, God's Spirit and the word of the Word Made Flesh come together or they do not come at all. Whoever hears believes. Whoever believes has the life of the age to come. Whoever resists and refuses does not see and so does not have the life that Jesus is and affords. God's wrath remains on him (3:36; cf. 1 John 5:11–12; and "see death," 8:51).[75]

---

72. The language of heaven above is only comprehensible to those who dwell in heaven. The language of the Godhead is only comprehensible to the persons of the Godhead.

73. Thus, the "lifting up" of the Son of Man, "acquires a double meaning here (as also in 8:28, 12:32, 35): the exaltation of the Son of [M]an (= his glorification) is effected by his being raised up on a cross" (Ridderbos, *John*, 136). See further 136–37.

74. Contrast the willingness of Abraham to offer up his one and only one (μονογενῆ), Isaac, in LXX Hebrews 11:17.

75. "Wrath" (ὀργή) appears only here in the Gospel and Letters of John.

CHAPTER THREE

A SECOND JOURNEY *to* JERUSALEM *in* ANTICIPATION *of the* COMING *of* HIS HOUR

John 4:1–5:47

In the story of Jesus that follows (4:1–5:47), Jesus goes to Jerusalem a second time. The days begin with his conversation with the Samaritan woman (4:1–30) and end again with reference to John (5:33–36). In these chapters, Jesus teaches that Spirit-wrought true worshipers worship the Father in response to the word of the Word Made Flesh who is the Truth or there is no opportunity for the human person to worship in Spirit and Truth (4:23–24). To thus honor the Father one must honor his exclusive agent (5:23). To honor his agent one must hear Jesus's word (5:24). To hear is to see. To see is even now to pass from death to life (5:24). The word of John was great (5:33). He was a bright shining light (5:35). But the word of the Word Made Flesh of whom Moses wrote (5:46) is even greater (5:36). Jesus is the one they must hear. Jesus is the one they must see.

On the one hand, the suggestion of a sharp contrast follows. The person and the conduct of the Samaritan woman contrast sharply with the person and previous conduct of Nicodemus. He is a man. She is a woman. He is a Jew. She is a Samaritan. He is a highly educated man of letters. He has all of the requisite degrees and is so highly regarded in the academy of his day that Jesus names him not a teacher but "*the* teacher of Israel" (3:10). He is a high and mighty "man of the Pharisees" and "ruler of the Jews" (3:1). So Nicodemus is also a sitting member of the Sanhedrin. He is the very model of an exceptionally prominent and extraordinarily respected Jew. She is not. She has had five previous husbands. And the man that she is with now is not her husband.[1] From the model Jewish man and what he represents in his world to the woman of Samaria and what she represents in hers, the polarities could not be more striking.

At the same time, what contributes to the tensions that inform the relationship of the two figures is not only the detail that distinguishes each from the other. Instead, what contributes also is what the two share in common. Like the rest of the Samaritans that she represents,[2] the Samaritan woman is more like her male counterpart and those that he represents than one might think. Like him, she too sees herself as a descendant of Abraham, Isaac, and Jacob (4:5, 6, 12).[3] She too believes that hers is the legacy of Israel's sons (4:12), especially of Israel's son Joseph (4:5). For the Samaritans held that they were the descendants and rightful heirs of the posterity of Joseph.[4] Therefore, she too awaits the coming of the prophet like Moses (Deut 18:15). Actually, on the basis of the only Scripture that the Samaritans were willing to recognize, the Five Books of Moses,[5] the Samaritans called their redeemer figure the Taheb, or Restorer.[6] But what the Samaritan woman otherwise shares with Nicodemus is, at least on the surface, the same Moses and the same promise of a prophet like Moses (4:19) who would be the

---

1. Cf. Jesus who is (3:29).

2. Cf. "our," 4:20; "you" (plural), 4:21, 22; and "us," 4:25. The Samaritans were a people of mixed ancestry. When the Assyrians conquered the Northern Kingdom in 722–721 BC, they brought colonists from five foreign nations to the region. See 2 Kings 17:24. See also Josephus, *Ant.* 9.288. In Jesus's day, the one that rules them is himself no legitimate heir of his throne. For the suggestion that the Samaritan woman's "personal history of marriage to five husbands and cohabitation with a sixth parallels the colonial history of Samaria," see Craig R. Koester, *Symbolism in the Fourth Gospel: Meaning, Mystery, Community*, 2nd ed. (Minneapolis: Fortress, 2003), 49. See further 47–50.

3. See further Mary L. Coloe, "The Woman of Samaria: Her Characterization, Narrative, and Theological Significance," in *Characters and Characterization in the Gospel of John*, ed. Christopher Skinner, LNTS 461 (London: Bloomsbury, 2012), 188–90.

4. See Koester, *Symbolism*, 49.

5. Cf. the five disciples of Jesus in 1:35–51 and the five previous husbands of the Samaritan woman in 4:18. See further the five porticoes of the pool Bethzatha at the Sheep Gate in 5:2–3, five barley breads for the five thousand who eat in 6:9–10, and the five of Israel who stand at the foot of the cross in 19:25–27.

6. See further what is known of the Samaritan hope in the "Taheb" or "Restorer" in Andreas Köstenberger, *John*, BECNT (Grand Rapids: Baker Academic, 2004), 157–58.

Messiah (4:25, 29; cf. 6:14). What the two share is the one of whom Moses wrote (1:45; 5:46).[7]

But in virtually every other personal and socioeconomic respect the woman of Samaria is the pronounced polar opposite of the very high and respected teacher of Israel (3:10). She is in many and various complicated ways a lowly, despised Samaritan (4:9). For the faith and hope of those she represents is, according to Jesus, a false hope. "You [plural] worship what you [plural] do not know," declares Jesus. But "we worship what we know."[8] For salvation is not of the Samaritans. Salvation (Messiah) is of the Jews (4:22). Great, then, is the ironic profundity of the moment when she, the damsel, the despised one, the model outsider, becomes what Nicodemus, the man of letters—the model insider—does not. Great irony results. For, in pointed, paradigmatic terms the Gospel's depiction of the Samaritan woman and of her manner of responding to the word of the Word Made Flesh is at first rather like the reaction of her counterpart. But then ultimately it fundamentally is not.

Like Nicodemus, the woman struggles mightily with the heavenly challenge of the earthly Jesus. Yet, unlike Nicodemus, she does not resist the word of the Word Made Flesh. Instead, she welcomes Jesus's promise of living water (ὕδωρ ζῶν, 4:10)[9] even when the meaning of his words is not yet clear.[10] Unlike Nicodemus, she responds positively when Jesus, who knows all things (2:24–25), shows again (cf. 1:48) that he miraculously knows the person with whom he is speaking (4:17–18; see also 4:29). Unlike Nicodemus, she responds with truths that are profoundly

---

7. For the figure of Moses in the Gospel of John, see further Stan Harstine, *Moses as a Character in the Fourth Gospel: A Study of Ancient Reading Techniques*, JSNTSup 229 (Sheffield: Sheffield Academic Press, 2002).

8. Here, "we" likely means the Jews. "Salvation" (σωτηρία) appears only here in the Gospel and Letters of John. Cf. "savior" (σωτήρ) in 4:42 and in 1 John 4:14.

9. Cf. "water which is the Spirit" in 3:5; and 7:38–39, where "rivers of living water" is explicitly interpreted as a reference to the Spirit. Here the water of which Jesus speaks is not a bath (2:6) but is instead a beverage that becomes in the one who drinks it "a spring of living water welling up to the life of the age to come" (4:14). Thus, it is a water that defines the recipient and is not described as a water that its recipients share with others. Jesus singularly bears and affords this in 7:37–38 and 19:34. See further "living bread" in 6:51; and "living Father" in 6:57.

10. Thus, over against Nicodemus before her, the Samaritan woman exhibits no greater understanding. Instead, she believes what she hears whether she understands it or not. Cf. the strikingly similar figure of the widow of Zarephath in 1 Kings 17:8–24, especially in v. 10, where, like Jesus (4:7), Elijah requests water from the widow.

greater than she knows. "Sir [χύριε]," declares the woman, "I perceive that you are a prophet!" (4:19).[11] Little does she know how right she really is. Unlike Nicodemus, even when the meaning of much of the word of the Word Made Flesh initially or entirely escapes her, she still takes his word to heart and believes it. Complete understanding is not necessary. What is necessary is a trusting willingness to wait on the promise of what is to come, whether one fully understands in the moment what that really is or not. And so, rather remarkably, she believes him when he says, "I am [he]" (ἐγώ εἰμι, 4:26). She believes him when he says that he is the Messiah (see 4:25). She who is initially sightless sees what Nicodemus, who thinks that he sees quite well (3:1–3), does not (cf. 9:39). She receives what he does not receive (3:11). She believes what he does not believe (3:12). By his word and by his word alone[12] she sees what he does not. For Spirit-wrought true worshipers worship the Father in response to the word of the Word Made Flesh, who is the Truth, or there is no opportunity for the human person to worship in Spirit and Truth (4:23–24).[13]

By the word of Jesus she comes to know him as her only true Husband.[14] By *her* word, "Come, see [cf. 1:39, 46] a man who told me everything that I have done" (4:29; see also 4:39), the Samaritans of that place believe also (4:39–40).[15] They beseech Jesus to stay with them for two more

---

11. The predicate nominative in 4:19 precedes the copula in the Greek and so may be construed as definite ("the prophet") rather than indefinite ("a prophet"). See also "when he [Messiah] comes, he will proclaim to us all things," 4:25. He will say what must be said. He will proclaim what must be heard.

12. There is no indication that Jesus performs a sign when he is with the Samaritans.

13. Again, he who is the latter bears the former (1:32) and is he who baptizes with it (1:33). See further on the Spirit of Truth in 14:17; 15:26; 16:13. See also 1 John 4:6; 5:6. Thus, "as the one who replaces the temple in Jerusalem," Jesus "also ends temple-situated worship whether in Jerusalem or in Gerizim and supplants it with worship 'in spirit and truth,'" (Ardel Caneday, "The Word Made Flesh as Mystery Incarnate: Revealing and Concealing Dramatized by Jesus as Portrayed in John's Gospel," *JETS* 60 [2017]: 761).

14. For the frequent suggestion that the initial controlling metaphor in John 4 is "one of betrothal in the most common of literary locales, a well" (see πηγή in 4:6; see also 4:14), see Bruce G. Schuchard, "The Wedding Feast at Cana and the Christological Monomania of St. John," in *All Theology is Christology: Essays in Honor of David P. Scaer*, ed. Dean O. Wenthe et al. (Fort Wayne, IN: Concordia Theological Seminary Press, 2000), 104 and 110–11 nn. 32–35, 41; and Coloe, "Woman of Samaria." See further the "well" in LXX Genesis 2:6.

15. Her cautiously worded yet hopeful question to them is "This one is not the Christ, is he?" (μήτι οὗτός ἐστιν ὁ χριστός, 4:29). "The form of the sentence," observes Brooke F. Westcott, "grammatically suggests a negative answer (v. 33), but hope bursts through it," see *The Gospel according to St. John: The Authorized Version with Introduction and Notes* (London: Murray, 1908; repr., Grand

days (4:40; see also 4:43). He does so. And even more come to believe in response to the word of the Word Made Flesh (4:41–42).[16] They take him at his word. As was significantly the case before (in 1:19–51) so also here, hearing without otherwise seeing alone prompts a believing and a confessing (4:42). Unlike his previous experience in the temple and with Nicodemus in the homeland (πατρίς)[17] of Israel's fathers, where a prophet even now has no honor (4:44), here Jesus is celebrated. Here they take the Word Made Flesh to be the "Savior of the World" (4:42).[18]

When Jesus's two days in Samaria come to an end, Jesus returns with his disciples to Galilee. There Jesus is enthusiastically received (4:43–45). But the enthusiasm of the Galileans is conspicuously again a believing in him on account of their previous seeing of his signs (4:45). Theirs is the ongoing previous reaction of the crowds (2:23–25). They too were at the feast (4:45). For this reason, an anonymous "royal one" (βασιλικός)[19] whose son is near death (4:46) comes from Capernaum (cf. 2:12). He finds Jesus who is again in Cana. And he begs Jesus to return with him to Capernaum so that Jesus might heal his son (4:46–47).

But Jesus knows that their believing in him solely on the basis of the signs lacks again what must finally inform it. So he upbraids them all for focusing only on his signs (4:48). No sufficiency will come if all they want and expect is more signs. No sufficiency will come if, in the absence of

---

Rapids: Eerdmans, 1981), 74. See further Köstenberger, *John*, 143, 159–60 (and those that he cites). Thus, she and many other Samaritans come to believe.

16. See especially their statement to her in 4:42: "We no longer believe on account of your speaking, for we ourselves have heard and know."

17. For the positions that have been taken in response to the use here of πατρίς, see Köstenberger, *John*, 168n4.

18. Köstenberger, *John*, 164–65, observes, "Interestingly, the OT never calls the Messiah 'savior,' " and so the expression apparently "was not a messianic title in first-century Judaism." Instead, the title "was applied to many Greek gods and Roman emperors, including Augustus (31 B.C.–A.D. 14), Tiberius (A.D. 14–37), and Nero (A.D. 54–68). According to Josephus, the emperor Vespasian (A.D. 69–79) was hailed upon his arrival in a given city as savior and benefactor ... and his son Titus (A.D. 79–81) received a similar welcome." Thus, "Savior of the World" constitutes a strong challenge to the imperial claims of the day. See the same in the analysis of "The One Who Is" in 1:18; and of "my Lord and my God" in 20:28.

19. "If this man was a Gentile, then this marks a progression from Jew (John 3) to Samaritan to Gentile (John 4) in Jesus' ministry, in keeping with the pattern followed also in the Book of Acts (cf. Acts 1:8)." The designation βασιλικός "usually refers to someone in the service of a king. In the present instance, the 'king' probably was Herod Antipas (cf. Mark 6:14), though Antipas technically did not hold that title, but rather was tetrarch of Galilee (4 B.C.–A.D. 39)." See Köstenberger, *John*, 169.

the signs, they refuse to believe. So Jesus responds with a challenge. He challenges them to do what they have not yet done. He challenges them to take him at his word. By his word alone does he heal. By his word alone does he make the sightless to see.[20] Therefore, he refuses the plaintive plea of the royal father (4:49) and instead challenges the man in the presence of them all to take Jesus at his word. "Go," declares Jesus, "your son lives!" (4:50).[21]

Remarkably, the man responds as desired. He takes Jesus at his word.[22] The man believes and goes on his way. Expecting no less, he departs. That the word of Jesus is worthy of the father's trust is confirmed later by the corroborating testimony of the servants of the man's household.[23] With the recovery of his son, his servants go out in search of their master to share the miraculous news. They meet him on his way home and tell him the news (4:51). The father inquires regarding the time of his son's recovery. And he hears that his son recovered *at the very hour* that Jesus had previously said to him, "Your son lives!" (4:52–53). That Jesus can and must be taken at his word is arrestingly affirmed. And the entire household of the grateful father believes also (4:53) when the man shares with his household his experience of the trustworthy word of the Word Made Flesh.[24]

Jesus returns with his disciples to Jerusalem for an additional but otherwise unidentified feast of the Jews (5:1). There, near the Sheep Gate[25] on the north side of the temple at the pool called Bethesda, he encounters a multitude. There under its roof supported by five colonnades he finds a multitude of those who are ailing for a variety of reasons (5:2–3).[26] He

---

20. What they hear must shape what they see. See Craig R. Koester, "Jesus' Resurrection, the Signs, and the Dynamics of Faith," in *The Resurrection of Jesus in the Gospel of John*, ed. Craig R. Koester and Reimund Bieringer, WUNT 222 (Tübingen: Mohr Siebeck, 2008), 54–55.

21. See also the very same "Your son lives" in LXX 1 Kings 17:23.

22. See "The man *believed the word* that Jesus spoke to him" in 4:50.

23. Likewise, Koester, *Symbolism*, 89.

24. Thus, "the story," observes Koester, "suggests that a faith based on hearing is the context within which Jesus' signs can rightly be perceived" (*Symbolism*, 89).

25. Cf. the Good Shepherd who enters by the gate to claim his sheep in 10:1–6.

26. "The sheep were washed in the pool before being taken to the sanctuary. This was also the place where invalids lay in hopes of being healed." In Aramaic, "Bethesda" may mean "house of mercy," "which would be a fitting term, given the desperate state of the people lying there in hope of miraculous healing" (Köstenberger, *John*, 178).

purposefully selects a man whose unidentified ailment has plagued him for thirty-eight years (5:5).[27] And Jesus asks him, "Do you wish to be well?" (5:6). But here in Israel's homeland where, again, the word of a prophet has even now no honor (4:44), the ailing one displays no knowledge of or interest in Jesus's ability to make him well. Instead, the man exhibits a profoundly misdirected interest in the presumed power of the pool and its water to make him well.[28] And so the man ironically says to Jesus, "Sir [κύριε], I have no one to cast me into the pool. When the water is stirred up, and while I am going, another goes down before me" (5:7).[29]

By the word of the Word Made Flesh[30] the Spirit that Jesus bears and confers does its work. By his word, Jesus who is the resurrection and the life (11:25) renews the life of the woefully unsuspecting man, saying, "Rise, take up your bed, and walk" (5:8). On the Sabbath (5:9), Jesus blesses him with a relief that he has not requested and does not expect to receive. Sadly, when healed, the healed one shows that—even then—he still has no knowledge of or concern for who Jesus is. When Jesus is no longer with him, and the Jews challenge him for taking up his bed in violation of the Sabbath (5:10), he suggests to them that the blame belongs to his

---

27. Cf. Israel's thirty-eight-year sojourn in the wilderness under Moses in LXX Deuteronomy 2:14. Contrast again the roof here supported by five colonnades with the five disciples of Jesus in 1:35–51; the five men/husbands of the Samaritan woman in 4:18 with the five nations that were made to populate Samaria after the exile of the Northern Kingdom; the fivefold Scripture of the Samaritans, which was the Five Books of Moses, with Jesus's suggestion that Moses in his Five Books "wrote about me" in 5:46; and the five breads made to feed five thousand in 6:9–10 with their resulting conclusion that Jesus is the prophet like Moses in 6:14–15 (cf. Deut 18:15: "him shall you hear"). Thus, Jesus gathers to himself a new people, a new Israel. See Schuchard, "Wedding Feast," 104. To be sure, he will do so especially "at the moment of the Gospel's τέλος (13:1; cf. 19:28–30), when five representatives of [the Testament of Moses]—when his mother, his mother's sister, Mary the wife of Clopas, Mary Magdalene, and the disciple whom he loved—are assembled at the cross." See further on the analysis of 19:25–27.

28. Again, without saying so, John's story seems to assume that its hearer would have known what motivated the multitude of those who were ailing to be at the pool. The secondary insertion of 5:3b–4 appearing only in later manuscripts of the Gospel offers the explanation that they were there "waiting for the moving of the water, for an angel of the Lord went down at certain seasons into the pool and stirred the water. Whoever stepped in first after the stirring of the water was healed of whatever disease he had."

29. The ailing one looks to the pool and its water, all the while neglecting in every way the healing power of the living water of God (7:37–39) that he who baptizes with the Holy Spirit (1:39) has come to provide. See Schuchard, "Wedding Feast," 111n37, for the suggestion that "what the sick man says about his inability to enter the pool is both right and wrong. Another must bear him. Indeed another must enter the troubled waters (of death) before him. Then the one can say to the other, 'Arise.' "

30. That "the mere word of Jesus sufficed" is noted by Köstenberger, *John*, 180.

healer. "The one who made me well," says the man, "that one said to me, 'Take up your bed and walk' " (5:11).[31] When asked, "Who is the person who said [this] to you?" (5:12), the man says that he does not know (5:13). Having received his well-being from him of whom the man expected it not, the man knows, and sees, nothing. The importance of the revelatory moment is entirely lost on the man.

Only later, when Jesus speaks with him again and upbraids him for failing to respond to Jesus as he should be responding,[32] does the man finally learn Jesus's name. "Behold," declares Jesus, "you are well. Sin no longer lest something worse [than your previous condition] happens to you" (5:14).[33] But the man fails again to respond as he should. Instead, he takes his leave and reports to the Jews "that it was Jesus who healed him" (5:15). Thus, he suggests again that the responsibility for what happened on the Sabbath lies with Jesus. It is Jesus who is to blame.[34] Though the man knows later who it was who came to his aid, in the end he has no enduring interest in Jesus (1:11).[35]

The charge of "doing these things on the Sabbath" (5:16) comes next to Jesus. When challenged to defend himself, he astounds his interlocutors with an inconceivable claim. Jesus claims that his sonship so surpasses theirs that who Jesus is as God's singular Son[36] makes it possible for Jesus to do whatever God does (5:17, 19).[37] Thus, Jesus claims that God is "his own Father" (5:18) in a way that they are not. Jesus's suggestion that he is not their equal astounds them. It enrages them. That Jesus is in this or

---

31. When reprimanded, "the man tries to evade responsibility by saying that he is only doing what he had been told, since his healer had directed him to carry the mat." See Craig R. Koester, *The Word of Life: A Theology of John's Gospel* (Grand Rapids: Eerdmans, 2008), 68.

32. Likewise, Koester, "Jesus' Resurrection," 59.

33. When Jesus suggests that something worse (χεῖρόν τι, 5:14) may befall the man, he refers to what will happen if the healed one persists in his failure to see Jesus as he must in the end be seen. See Koester, *Word of Life*, 68.

34. See again Koester, *Word of Life*, 68.

35. See further Köstenberger, *John*, 183, and those that he cites.

36. See elsewhere the analysis of 1:14, 18; 3:16, 18.

37. See Koester, *Symbolism*, 91–92.

in any other sense "equal to God" (5:18) is the worst sort of blasphemy.[38] Jesus should therefore die.[39] And yet Jesus persists and says even more.

Such equality means that Jesus does nothing on his own. Instead, he does only what his Father does (5:19) so that others may then see. To be sure, even greater works than these works will they see (5:20). For just as the Father raises the dead and gives life to the world so also does Jesus (5:21). All judgment the Father likewise gives to the Son (5:22) so that all may honor the Son just as they honor the Father (5:23). To honor the Father one must honor his agent (5:23). To honor the agent one must hear the word of the Word Made Flesh.[40] Only "the one who hears [ὁ ἀκούων] and believes [καὶ πιστεύων]" has what Christ alone proffers (5:24).[41]

To hear is to see. To see is even now to pass from death to life.[42] To be sure, a long-awaited hour (ὥρα) is coming and is even now present in Jesus when those who are dead will hear God's Voice in the voice of the Word Made Flesh. And those who hear will live (5:25). For just as the Father has life in himself so also has he granted the Son to have life in himself. And the Father has given his Son authority to execute judgment because his Son is the[43] Son of Man (5:26-27). Indeed, an hour is coming and is now present when all who are in the tombs will hear Jesus's

---

38. Cf. the desire of Adam and Eve to be like God in Genesis 3:5.

39. "By now, the issue of Sabbath observance (dealt with further in 7:19-24) has been dwarfed by the question of Jesus' relationship with God"(Köstenberger, *John*, 185). Their charge that with his words he was making himself equal to God will be the same charge that later leads to his crucifixion.

40. "To hear God was the defining habitus of Israel; to be Israel was to hear God and do what one heard (Ex 3:14-18; contrast Ex 4:1)." See again Deuteronomy 6:4. Therefore, the words of Jesus "define that person who belongs to the new Israel. He who belongs to the new Israel is he who 'hears my word and believes him who sent me' (Jn 5:24)." See William C. Weinrich, *John 1:1-7:1*, ConcC (St. Louis: Concordia, 2015), 594.

41. See Charles K. Barrett, *The Gospel according to St. John*, 2nd ed. (Philadelphia: Westminster, 1978), 261, who notes here the important pairing of the participles for hearing and believing, which combine to describe the singular reality of a person who hears *and* believes (see also 5:38). The latter happens only as does the former. To hear is to believe. To believe is to see what unaided, mere mortal, flesh-and-blood eyes can in no way see.

42. "The pronouncement represents one of the strongest affirmations of realized (inaugurated) eschatology in John's Gospel." See Köstenberger, *John*, 188.

43. The predicate nominative precedes the copula in the Greek and so may be construed as definite ("the Son") rather than indefinite ("a Son"). For the unusual absence of an article before both "Son" and "Man" (similarly, see Rev 1:13; 14:14) and the possibility that the result contributes to the strong suggestion of an allusion to the same combination in Daniel 7:13, see Köstenberger, *John*, 189, and those that he cites.

voice. And they will come out either to the resurrection of life or to the resurrection of judgment (5:28–29; cf. 10:3; 11:43–44). Dry bones will hear. And those who by the Spirit hear will see. And those who by the Spirit see will live.[44] For "as the *Word* Incarnate, Jesus speaks with a voice beyond which there is no voice."[45] Only in the resurrection when the voice of Jesus is finally heard as God's very own Voice will Jesus's words inform (2:22; see also 8:28; 12:16) and his form be seen as that of the God who must be seen (1:18).[46]

Jesus's discourse and his second trip to Jerusalem end, as does his first, with reference to John. They end also with reference to the preeminent witness of Moses. The witness of John, like that of Jesus, was not his own. Instead, it too was nothing more than what he was sent to say. John was a lesser light (5:35; cf. Ps 132:17). Jesus is *the* Light. Many were willing to hear first from John. But the word of the Word Made Flesh is greater. Everything the Word Made Flesh is and says and otherwise does is revelatory. They are all "works" that reveal (5:36).[47] Yet only his spoken word is sufficient to inform what must be informed. The Father that the opponents of Jesus have never seen or heard bears witness to Jesus (5:37).[48] But the word of the Father is not in them because the word of Jesus is not in them. For the word of the Father and the word of the Word Made Flesh are one and the same (5:38). Others may claim the Scriptures, but the Scriptures bear witness to Jesus (5:39). Jesus comes in his Father's name (5:43). But others refuse him. They refuse the glory that comes alone

---

44. Cf. the speaking of the Creator in Genesis 1–2. See also Revelation 1:3; Deuteronomy 32:1; Isaiah 1:2. "Again the language of creation appears," observes Weinrich, "for in speaking his word Jesus speaks into existence something new"—namely, "a man who lives from the word of the Word (cf. Deut 8:3). He who is the Word (ὁ λόγος, Jn 1:1, 14) speaks the word (τὸν λόγον, Jn 5:24). What does this mean other than that he speaks what he was incarnated to effect in those paralyzed by sin and destined to death." See *John 1:1–7:1*, 593–94.

45. Weinrich, *John 1:1–7:1*, 600.

46. Cf. "his voice you have never heard, his form you have never seen" in 5:37 and the formless one who does not speak in Rev 4:2–3.

47. "Thus, his works include the signs but are not limited to them. Everything Jesus does, or even says," even "his entire ministry" is to be included in "what constitutes his 'works' " (Köstenberger, *John*, 192).

48. In what sense this witness has happened or will happen is less than clear. See, however, the Father's sending of the Son to whom he delegates all things in 5:36; his sealing of the Son in 6:27; his drawing of others to the Son in 6:44; his glorifying the Son in 8:54 (see also 12:28; 17:5, 24); and his giving of the Spirit of Truth so that those who believe may know the Truth that Jesus is in 14:16–17, 26; 15:26; 16:13.

from him (5:44). "How can you believe?" asks Jesus. There is no other way. The presumptive focus of their hope has become their accuser (5:45). They have failed to hear Moses. Faith in Moses means faith in Jesus. For Moses wrote of him (5:46). Faith in Moses means that one must believe the word of the Word Made Flesh (5:47).[49]

49. See Köstenberger, *John*, 195.

CHAPTER FOUR

A THIRD JOURNEY *to* JERUSALEM *in* ANTICIPATION *of the* COMING *of* HIS HOUR

John 6:1–10:42

In the story of Jesus that follows (6:1–10:42), Jesus goes to Jerusalem a third time. The days begin with Jesus's feeding of the five thousand (6:1–13) and end with a final reference to John (10:41–42). In these chapters, Jesus emphatically declares that his words are Spirit and life (6:63). But many of his own disciples find his words impossible to hear (6:60). And they abandon him (6:66). Only the Twelve do what is necessary. Only the Twelve take him at his word. They believe him even when he speaks truths that are greater than they are in a position to see. To those who abide a day of greater clarity will come (8:31–32). But many are unable to do this. Jesus comes to give sight to the sightless (9:39). But the sightless must hear the voice of the Good Shepherd (10:3–5), or they will never see. With such themes, the first half of the Gospel (1:19–10:42) comes to an end. Solely sufficient testimony is given that later must inform the accomplishment of Jesus's hour, that later must inform his person and work, if any are to see Jesus as he must in the end be seen. Jesus and his disciples go away again across the Jordan to the place where John previously was (10:40). Many follow Jesus. They recall the truth of John's words (10:41). And they believe (10:42).

Themes indicative of Moses and of Israel's experience of Moses continue to punctuate what follows.[1] A sea is mentioned (6:1) that later Jesus and his disciples will cross (6:16–21). The name of a present overlord to whom Israel is currently subject is given (6:1). Many follow Jesus in response to his signs (6:2). Jesus and those with him are at a mountain (6:3). The second of the Gospel's three Passovers is near (6:4; cf. 2:13, 23). Jesus feeds the multitude that is there. A child's[2] five barley breads[3] and two fish[4] (6:9) feed five thousand men (6:10).[5] Jesus instructs his disciples to gather and to keep what remains (6:12). The result is twelve baskets full of bread (6:13), one in the hands of each of the Twelve.[6] When all

---

1. To be sure, for Richard B. Hays, "the identity-defining Exodus narrative hovers constantly in the background of John's story." *Echoes of Scripture in the Gospels* (Waco: Baylor University Press, 2016), 301.

2. In the LXX, "child" (παιδάριον) describes Abraham's beloved (cf. MT: "only") son, when the Angel of the Lord prevents Abraham from sacrificing Isaac in Genesis 22:11–12 and says, "Lay not your hand upon the child and do not do anything to him, for now I know that you fear God and have not spared your beloved son on account of me." It also describes Joseph when his brothers who despise him attempt to kill him in Genesis 37:29–39; 42:22.

3. For "barley bread" (κρίθινος ἄρτος) as the bread of the poor, see Andreas Köstenberger, *John*, BECNT (Grand Rapids: Baker Academic, 2004), 201n14. See further Elisha in LXX 2 Kings 4:42–44.

4. The total number of food items is seven. The term here for "fish" (ὀψάριον) appears elsewhere in the Greek of the LXX and New Testament only in 6:11 and three times in 21:9, 10, 13. The term common to the rest of the NT (ἰχθύς) appears in John only three times in 21:6, 8, 11. See further on the analysis of 21:1–14.

5. The text mentions only the number of the men. "Man" (ἀνήρ) appears elsewhere in the works of John only in 1:13 and 30 (where the focus is the one and only opportunity that we have to be born of God through the man, Jesus); 4:16–18 (five times, where the question is who is and who is not the true man of the Samaritan woman who has had five previous men, but the one that she has now is not her "man"); and in Revelation 21:2 (where the Holy City, new Jerusalem, comes down out of heaven as a bride prepared and adorned for her man).

6. Accordingly, they are for the first time called the Twelve in 6:67, 70, 71 (three times). Thus, the disciples, observes Köstenberger, "form the core" of that "new messianic community" that will be the *new Israel* (*John*, 203). See also Bruce G. Schuchard, "The Wedding Feast at Cana and the Christological Monomania of St. John," in *All Theology is Christology: Essays in Honor of David P. Scaer*, ed. Dean O. Wenthe et al. (Fort Wayne, IN: Concordia Theological Seminary Press, 2000), 111n39, recalling Did. 9:4: "As this broken bread was scattered over the hills, and then, when gathered, became one loaf, so may your church be gathered from the ends of the earth into your kingdom." See further the 144,000 (twelve times 12,000) sealed ones "from every tribe of the sons of Israel" in Revelation 7:4–8; the "woman clothed with the sun, with the moon under her feet, and on her head a crown of twelve stars" and her children who are "those who hold to the testimony of Jesus" in Revelation 12:1–17; the Bride, the Wife of the Lamb, which is the new Jerusalem in Revelation 21:9–21, whose twelve gates are twelve pearls bearing twelve angels and are each inscribed with one of the twelve "names of the twelve tribes of the sons of Israel," whose twelve foundations are inscribed with "the twelve names of the twelve apostles of the Lamb," whose foursquare length and width is 12,000 stadia long, and whose walls are 144 (12 times 12) cubits thick; and "the tree of life with its twelve kinds of fruit, yielding its fruit each month" of the twelve-month-long year in Revelation 22:2.

of this happens, those fed fail to see rightly.[7] They see a prophet (6:14). They see a king (6:15).[8] But Jesus declines their desire to make him their king, and he separates himself from them all. For Jesus knows what limits their thinking and befouls their expectation.

The next morning, many who were fed follow Jesus to Capernaum (6:22–25). The experience of the previous day has them thinking that what he then gave he, like Moses before him, should be ready to give over and over again. But this is not why Jesus has come. He therefore seeks to inform what they should have seen.[9] He says, "Truly, truly, I say to you, you seek me not because you saw signs," not because they saw what they should have seen when previously they saw the sign. Instead, you are here, suggests Jesus, "because you ate of the breads and had your fill" (6:26).[10] To see rightly is to see that Jesus has come to be and to do far more than they are imagining. Jesus therefore exhorts them to work not for more of the same but for a greater food that will endure in the age that is to come. For this is what the Son of Man who bears God's seal has come to be and to do (6:27). He therefore challenges them to believe in and thus to receive the one that God has sent (6:28–29). For he is himself the very food of which he speaks.[11]

"To work for" is "to believe" (6:29).[12] To believe is to receive not some of what Jesus is but all of what he is. Ironically, they unwittingly attempt to strike a bargain with Jesus. They will gladly do what Jesus says if he gives

---

7. See also the incomprehension of his followers in 6:5–9.

8. See Craig R. Koester, *Symbolism in the Fourth Gospel: Meaning, Mystery, Community*, 2nd ed. (Minneapolis: Fortress, 2003), 95–97. See further the linking of prophet (like Moses) and king in Bruce G. Schuchard, *Scripture within Scripture: The Interrelationship of Form and Function in the Explicit Old Testament Citations in the Gospel of John*, SBLDS 133 (Atlanta: Scholars Press, 1992), 41–42.

9. Cf. what they see in 6:22 when "the crowd that stood on the other side of the sea *saw* that there had been only one boat there, and that Jesus had not entered the boat with his disciples, but that his disciples had gone away alone." None of this did they see with their eyes. A day later, this is what they somehow discovered (heard from others?) in the absence of Jesus and his disciples.

10. See further in greater detail the exchange that follows in Schuchard, *Scripture within Scripture*, 38–46.

11. For this reason, the previous day's leftovers in 6:12–13 are gathered up "so that nothing may be lost." Instead, they become the responsibility of those whose trust will later be to "feed my sheep" (21:15–17).

12. Jesus therefore clarifies what it means to eat and to drink when he states, "The one who *comes to me* shall in no way hunger [οὐ μὴ πεινάσῃ], and the one who *believes in me* shall in no way at any time thirst [οὐ μὴ διψήσει πώποτε]" (6:35).

them more to see (6:30). After all, does not the Scripture say of Israel's
fathers who were in the wilderness for forty years, "He gave them bread
from heaven to eat" (6:31)? Should not, then, the previous day's sign be
one that similarly repeats itself?[13] But more of what he formerly gave them
will not help them see what they are failing to see. More of the same was
not the preceding day's point. Neither was it the purpose of the manna
in the wilderness.[14] He has not come to provide them with a steady diet
of perishable and perishing things (6:27). Therefore, as he has before (cf.
2:18–19), Jesus declines their interest and instead speaks to what they
should have seen in their experience of him that they are still failing to see.

Properly speaking, Moses did not previously give, adds Jesus. Instead,
the Father did so (6:32). Therefore, the same Father gives even now. And
what he gives is Jesus. What he gives is later and greater *true Bread* for the
life of the world in fulfillment of both his prior giving and that of Jesus.
When the time comes for the accomplishment of Jesus's hour, Jesus will
depart this world (by means of his death).[15] But he will not depart never
to return. He will instead return (by means of his resurrection).[16] He
will return so that his solely sufficient revelatory word might allay fear,
enlighten eyes (2:22; see also 8:28; 12:16), and transport those who are
his own to where they and he will dwell as one forever (cf. 14:2–3; 17:24).[17]

---

13. For their expectation that with the coming of Messiah God's people would again be blessed with bread from heaven to eat, see 2 Baruch 29:8. See also Sib. Or. 3:49. See further Revelation 2:17.

14. After all, suggests Jesus, "your fathers ate the manna in the wilderness and died" (6:49). "Jesus refers to unfaithful Israel," which "did not hearken to the voice of God, and so they died. He speaks as well of the new Israel, which he himself is, for he is that man who is perfectly conformed to God's Word because he is the Word of God made flesh (Jn 1:14). 'Hear, O Israel, the Lord, our God, the Lord is one!' (Deut 6:4; cf. Jn 8:26, 29, 38). As the new Israel, Jesus has been sent so that in him also others might become members of the new Israel." See William C. Weinrich, *John 1:1–7:1*, ConcC (St. Louis: Concordia, 2015), 700.

15. See his foreshadowing comments regarding his imminent departure that will come with the day that he dies in 7:33–36; 8:21–23; 14:2, 4–5, 12; 16:5–7.

16. See also his attempts to assure his followers of his intention to return to them on the day of his resurrection in 14:3, 18–19; 16:16–22.

17. Similarly, see in the foreshadowing detail of the crossing of the sea in 6:16–21 a last hour before sunset (ὀψία; cf. Matt 16:2; Mark 1:32) followed by darkness, and Jesus is absent; the disciples are alone; the disciples fear for their lives; Jesus returns to the disciples but at first they are not comprehending and instead fear; his revelatory word allays their fear; they rejoice; and "immediately" they with Jesus are miraculously "at the land to which they were going." Thus, the "focal point of the episode is not the act of walking but the act of speaking" in response to a circumstance "which might suggest something about the dangers of separation from Jesus" (Koester, *Symbolism*, 97, 152).

Jesus previously gave them bread (cf. the manna). He also gave them meat (cf. the quail).[18] For the bread that Jesus will give for the life of the world is his very own flesh (6:51; cf. 1:14), *his flesh for all flesh*. He gives so that all who are of the flesh (3:6) might share in his own flesh[19] and, doing so, live. To hear is to come. To come is to believe (6:29, 35, 37, 45). To believe is to receive not some of him but all of him (6:27–29, 35, 53–56). Only those who thus eat and drink will live.[20] Only those who thus see and believe will see and be as is he.[21] Sadly, those hearing Jesus see but do not see. They see but do not believe (6:36). They hear but choke on his words. They do not see him. All they see is the earthly son of an earthly father and mother (6:42; cf. 1:45). All they hear is talk of an earthly, abhorrent eating and drinking (6:52).[22] The Father in heaven above draws to himself through his Mouth, Jesus (6:44). They must thus be *taught by God* (6:45). They must hear and learn, or never will they learn. No one has ever seen the Father (1:18a; 5:37). Only Jesus sees (6:46). Only Jesus knows. Only Jesus speaks of what they must know. Such things can only

---

See further on many of the same elements in the analysis of the disciples' experience of the death of Jesus and of Jesus's returning to them in 20:1, 8, 16–17, 19–23, 26–29; 21:1–14.

18. See Exodus 16:13; Numbers 11:31; Numbers 11:32; Psalm 105:40.

19. For "flesh and blood" as a "Hebrew idiom referring to the whole person" (Matt 16:17; 1 Cor 15:50; Gal 1:16; Eph 6:12; Heb 2:14), see Köstenberger, John, 216.

20. Here, to eat is to live. Contrast LXX Genesis 2:16–17 and 3:1–24, where Adam and Eve eat and die.

21. See Craig R. Koester, *The Word of Life: A Theology of John's Gospel* (Grand Rapids: Eerdmans, 2008), 88, 207–9. For by his extraordinary grace the one who believes has even now the totality of who Jesus is and what Jesus gives (6:47) not only in, with, and under the bread and the wine of the Supper of our Lord but ever and always, or one has him not at all. See 1 John 3:1–2. See also Colossians 3:4. What one therefore is in the not yet (see the eating and the drinking in Rev 19:6–9) one is even now as one awaits the manifest experience of the same in the experience of the not yet or one receives him not (1:11). By his grace with eyes of faith that he gives us now we know not that we will *become* this but that we *are* this even now. Though none of this is as yet manifest, still by grace through faith we see what at the present time unaided, mere mortal, flesh-and-blood eyes can in no way see. We therefore know that when he appears the true nature of our participation in him will do so also. When he appears we will finally see in all of its manifest fullness the eating and the drinking that is he in us and we in him (6:56). We will see that we have thus been made to be just like him, for we shall see him just as he is, as he is in us and we are in him.

22. Because "unbelief cannot see the revelation in its reality because it is oriented toward that reality which is earthly and visible, unbelief mistakes the true essence of Jesus and loses as well his gift of salvation," observes Ulrich Wilckens *Das Evangelium nach Johannes*, 17th ed., NTD 4 (Göttingen: Vandenhoeck & Ruprecht, 1998), 103. Concurring, Weinrich cites Augustine (*Tractate* 26.1.1 [FC 79:259]), who writes, "They had weak jaws of the heart; they were deaf with open ears; they saw and stood blind" (*John 1:1–7:1*, 698n17).

be known through the word of the Word Made Flesh. It is he alone who thus makes God known (1:18b).[23]

"When one acknowledges the eternal voice which is heard with the ear to be the Father's merciful and gracious voice,"[24] only then is one taught by God. Only then does one see. Sadly, they see and hear but recoil in horror at his words and refuse to believe. They see but do not see because they are unwilling, they are unable, to hear. "His *words* are hard words," say many of his own disciples. "Who is able to listen?" (6:60). "Do you take offense at my *words*?" asks Jesus (6:61). What if he gave them what they want? Would it help if he gave them more to see? "What if you were to *see* the Son of Man ascending to where he was before?" asks Jesus (6:62). Would that help? Sadly, it will not. They will never see if they continue to refuse what they must hear to inform what they must see.

The Spirit gives life. The *words* of the Word Made Flesh are Spirit and life (6:63).[25] But many of his disciples find his words impossible to hear (6:60). So they abandon him (6:66). Remarkably and tellingly, only the Twelve do what is necessary. Only the Twelve take him at his word, even when he speaks truths that are greater than they are in a position to see. Even so, as all ultimately must, they take his word to heart and believe it even when they do not entirely comprehend it.[26] In fact, both wittingly and unwittingly they believe and confess that the word of Jesus is supremely important. Speaking for the others,[27] Peter responds to Jesus who asks if they too are about to depart (6:67). "Lord, to whom shall *we* go?" asks Peter. "You have the words of the life of the age that is to come.

---

23. Therefore, when God promises Moses that he "will raise up for them a prophet like you from among their brothers" (Deut 18:18), he likewise declares, "And I will put my words in his mouth, and he shall speak to them all that I instruct him. And whoever will not listen to my words that he shall speak in my name, I myself will require it of him" (Deut 18:18–19). Thus, God's provision of the manna through Moses was itself given so that Israel might know "that man does not live by bread alone, but man lives by every word that comes from the mouth of the Lord" (Deut 8:3).

24. Weinrich, *John 1:1–7:1*, 716.

25. See further the life that the Spirit gives through the word in Köstenberger, *John*, 219–20.

26. Thus, believing involves "acceptance of Jesus and willingness to remain with him despite difficulties of all kinds, including uncertainty about precisely what it is that Jesus is revealing." See Kelli S. O'Brien, "Written That You May Believe: John 20 and Narrative Rhetoric," *CBQ* 67 (2005): 291.

27. Likewise, Koester, *Symbolism*, 70. See further the one contributing to the portrait of the many in Susan Hylen, "The Disciples: The 'Now' and the 'Not Yet' of Belief in Jesus," in *Character Studies in the Fourth Gospel: Narrative Approaches to Seventy Figures in John*, ed. Steven A. Hunt et al. (Grand Rapids: Eerdmans, 2013), 214–27.

And *we* have believed and have come to know that you are the Holy One of God" (6:68–69).[28]

Sadly, the crisis of confidence that many experienced in Capernaum in response to Jesus's words was shared by others. Later, Jesus's very own brothers (i.e., the sons of Joseph and Mary according to the flesh)[29] show that they too have had enough. They too are gravely disenchanted. So they confront their brother regarding the unwelcome, seemingly unending challenge of finding a meaningful direction in the vexing mystery of his words and deeds. They challenge him to get on with it lest they give up on it and leave him as so many have already done. They want actions, not words. They want Jesus to become the evident fulfillment of Israel's hope. He needs to stop holding them all hostage (cf. 10:24). The Feast of Tabernacles is coming soon (7:1–4).[30] Jesus needs to return to Judea to give to all who are there something to see. It is time for Jesus to show himself not just to them but to all the world (7:4). Their ultimatum is deeply distressing. For, at this point in their experience of him, "not even his [own] brothers believed in him" (7:5).

As he has with others, so also here, Jesus declines them (7:6–8). He declines and delays (7:9; cf. 11:6). Only later does he go up to the feast, not on their terms but on his own terms (7:10). And then he does exactly what they do not want him to do (7:14). In the middle of the feast, he proceeds again in the temple to teach all who are present what they must do if any are ever to see. Appropriately enough, those present marvel at his teaching and say, "How does this one know the Scriptures, when he

---

28. Peter likely speaks again a truth that is greater than any of them are in a position to know when he notably declares not that they have come to know and so they believe but they have believed and so they know. See further on the analysis of 20:29. Yet one of them is also "a/the devil" (6:70). The predicate nominative precedes the copula in the Greek and so may be construed as definite ("the devil") rather than indefinite ("a devil").

29. See 7:3, 5, 10. See elsewhere the Gospel's only other reference to the sons of Joseph and Mary according to the flesh in 2:12. Like their mother and the Beloved Disciple, the brothers are never named. Neither is the sister of their mother named (19:25). Cf. their father in 1:45 and 6:42, whose name is recalled but who does not otherwise appear in the Gospel's telling of its story.

30. See Koester, *Symbolism*, 156–59, 192–200. The "theme underlying Tabernacles" was that of Isaiah 12:3: "With joy you will draw from the wells of salvation" (Köstenberger, *John*, 226). See further 12:6: "for great in your midst is the Holy One of Israel"; 44:3: "For I will pour water on the thirsty land, and streams on the dry ground; I will pour my Spirit upon your offspring, and my blessing on your descendants"; 55:1: "Come, everyone who thirsts, come to the waters; and he who has no money, come ... buy wine ... without money and without price"; 58:11: "and you will be like a watered garden, like a spring of water, whose waters do not fail." See also 35:6–7; 41:17; 43:20; 49:10.

has not pursued [their formal] study?" (7:15). Once more, Jesus responds, saying, "My teaching is not my own, but is his who sent me" (7:16). To do God's will one must hear Jesus (7:17). To refuse is to decline even more than they are imagining. Not only do they disavow Moses (7:19–24). They disavow God.

Jesus upbraids them for their failure to do what they must, for judging by appearances (7:24) and not by the word of the Word Made Flesh. He admonishes them for not hearing what they at the same time are unable to refute (7:26). Instead, they rather feebly continue to ponder the seemingly imponderable. How can this Jesus be the Christ? After all, "when the Christ appears, no one will know where he comes from" (7:27). Yet they wrongly think that they know whence this one comes (1:45–46; 7:41). In reality, they know neither Jesus nor the one who sent him (7:28). Because some continue to believe on account of his signs (7:31), Jesus points again to what they are still failing to see in his signs. Doing so, he says also for the first time that he is soon to depart this world (7:33–34). They, however, fail again to comprehend his words (7:35–36). They fail to see what can only be seen by the one who hears his word.

On the last, great day of the feast,[31] Jesus stands up and cries out, "If anyone thirsts, let the one who believes in me come to me and drink" (7:37–38).[32] "As the Scripture has said," adds Jesus, "Out of his [i.e., my] belly[33]

---

31. "Every day during Tabernacles," observes Köstenberger, "priests marched in solemn procession from the pool of Siloam to the temple and poured out [Siloam's] water at the base of the altar. The seventh day of the festival, the last day proper (Lev. 23:34, 41–42), was marked by a special water-pouring rite and light ceremony (*m. Sukkah* 4.1, 9–10). This was to be followed by a sacred assembly on the eighth day, which was set apart for sacrifices, the joyful dismantling of the booths, and repeated singing of the Hallel (Ps. 113–18)" (*John*, 239). "The eighth day of this feast was also the last festival day in the Jewish year. Philo (*Spec. Laws* 2.33 §213) speaks of it as 'a sort of complement … and conclusion of all the feasts in the year' " (n51).

32. The grammar of 7:37–38 is much debated. Either ὁ πιστεύων εἰς ἐμέ (the one who believes in me) at the beginning of 7:38 is a fronted pendant element in the sentence that follows and specifies first the identity of the one from whom rivers of living water will flow, or the same words are the subject of the two third-person imperatives ἐρχέσθω (let [him] come) and πινέτω (let [him] drink) in the sentence that precedes in 7:37. The latter is alone likely. Never does Scripture elsewhere suggest that rivers of living water will flow from the believer ("welling up" in 4:14 suggests instead that the living water that Jesus [alone!] gives will fill in every way and so benefit the one who receives and believes). Jesus speaks of himself.

33. See elsewhere John's only other use of κοιλία (belly) in 3:4; and Revelation 10:9–10. Cf. the "belly" of David in LXX Psalm 131:11.

rivers[34] of *living water*[35] will flow" (7:38).[36] Now Jesus said this "concerning *the Spirit*" (7:39).[37] But again they fail to comprehend the word of the
Word Made Flesh. "For as yet the Spirit was not, because Jesus was not yet
glorified" (7:39).[38] So, again, his word fails to enlighten their eyes. Instead,
it divides them. Some say, "This truly is the prophet!" (7:40). Others say,
"This is the Christ!" (7:41a). But many continue to ironically ponder what
they think they happen to know.[39] "Is the Christ to come from Galilee?"
they ask (7:42b). "Has not the Scripture said that the Christ comes from
the offspring of David and from Bethlehem, the village where David was?"
(7:42).[40] They see but do not see. The problem is his word (7:43).

---

34. See elsewhere John's only other use of ποταμός (river) in Revelation, especially Revelation
22:1–2: "Then the angel showed me the river of the water of life, bright as crystal, flowing from the
throne of God and of the Lamb through the middle of the street of the city; also, on either side of the
river, the tree of life with its twelve kinds of fruit, yielding its fruit each month. The leaves of the tree
were for the healing of the nations." See further the similarity of what Ezekiel sees in Ezekiel 47:1–12.

35. For the tradition that the Jerusalem temple lay on the wellspring of the earth, the center and
source of the life-giving water of Genesis 2:6–7, see Coloe, "Woman of Samaria," 186–88.

36. Similarly, see Hays, *Echoes*, 314–16. See also Andrew T. Lincoln, *Truth on Trial: The Lawsuit
Motif in the Fourth Gospel* (Peabody, MA: Hendrickson, 2000), 52–54; Francis J. Moloney, *John*,
SP 4 (Collegeville, MN: Liturgical Press, 1998), 256 (and those he cites); and Johannes Beutler, *A
Commentary on the Gospel of John*, trans. Michael Tait (Grand Rapids: Eerdmans, 2017), 222–24.
Cf. the rock in the wilderness in LXX Isaiah 48:21: "And if they thirst, he will lead them through
the desert. He will bring forth water for them out of the rock. The rock will be split, and water will
flow [ῥυήσεται], and my people will drink." The verb "flow" that Isaiah 48:21 and John 7:38 share
appears nowhere else in the New Testament. See further LXX Psalm 104:41: "He split a rock, and
waters flowed [ἐρρύησαν], rivers [ποταμοί] ran in dry places" (cf. LXX Ps 77:16, 20; 113:8; 147:7; Joel
4:18; Zech 14:8). See also the lament of the suffering servant in LXX Psalm 21:15: "I am poured out
like water ... my heart has become like wax that is melting in the midst of my belly [κοιλίας]"; and
21:1: "O God, my God ... why have you forsaken me" (cf. Matt 24:6; Mark 15:34); 21:17: "they have
pierced my hands and my feet" (cf. Luke 24:39–40; see also John 20:20, 25, 27); 21:19: "they divided
my garments among them, and for my clothing they cast lots" (cf. John 19:24). "The festival seems
to speak of the joyful restoration of Israel and the ingathering of the nations," observes Köstenberger,
John, 240. "Here Jesus presents himself as God's agent to make these end-time events a reality." Cf.
the thinking of Paul in 1 Corinthians 10:1–4: "For I do not want you to be unaware, brothers, that our
fathers were all under the cloud, and all passed through the sea, and all were baptized into Moses in
the cloud and in the sea, and all ate the same spiritual food, and all drank the same spiritual drink.
For they drank from the spiritual Rock that followed them, and the Rock was Christ."

37. Cf. water that is the Spirit in Isaiah 44:3; Ezekiel 36:25–27. See also "one of the soldiers pierced
his side [πλευράν] with a spear, and immediately blood and water came out," 19:34. See elsewhere
John's only other use of πλευρά (side) in 20:20, 25, 27 (three times).

38. See further the death of Jesus as the day of his glorification (the day that he will impart the
Spirit "without measure," 3:34) in 12:16, 23, 28; 13:31; 17:1, 5. Cf. the death of Peter as that which will
also glorify in 21:19.

39. See Koester, *Word of Life*, 93–94.

40. Thus, the text here "assumes that readers would know the tradition about Jesus' birth in
Bethlehem" (Koester, *Symbolism*, 154).

Officers sent by the chief priests and Pharisees to seize Jesus do not seize him (7:44). So, later, the officers are asked, "Why did you not bring him?" (7:45). They respond with a truth that is greater than they know, saying, "No one has ever *spoken* like this one" (7:46). The deception of the Pharisees is glaringly great. Yet the Pharisees ironically accuse the officers of sharing in the deception of the masses (7:47, 49). Nicodemus, who previously was neither receiving nor believing (3:11–12), appears again. This time, Nicodemus offers the ironically sympathetic statement that, according to the law, this Jesus should receive a fair hearing. Only then can anyone know what must be known (7:50–51). But the Pharisees repudiate Nicodemus as well, saying, "Are you also from Galilee? Search and see that no prophet rises from Galilee" (7:52). They presume to see quite well both the man and the matter. But they show that they are actually blind to the truth of who Jesus is or why he has come. Such things can only be seen by the one takes him at his word.

No suggestion of a change in location or audience is given. Therefore, seemingly still at the feast,[41] Jesus testifies further to the critical importance of the word of the Word Made Flesh. He speaks to an apparently mixed crowd of both friends and foes. And before them he declares that he is the Light of the World. "Whoever follows me," he says, "will not walk in darkness but will have the light of life" (8:12). For the word of the Word Made Flesh is light and life. But, again, neither his friends nor his foes comprehend his words. And so he declares, "I know where I have come from. But you do not know where I come from [who he truly is; cf. 7:27–29] or where I am going [what he has come to be and to do]" (8:14). The testimony of the Father in and through his Son is true (8:17). But the word of Jesus is too hard for them (cf. 6:60–66). Therefore, they fail to see what must be seen (1:18) in what they have thus far seen. They fail to know Jesus. So they fail also to know the Father who dwells in heaven above.[42]

Again, Jesus declares that he is soon to depart (cf. 7:33–34). "I am going away," he says. "And you will seek me," but "where I am going, you cannot come" (8:21). Again, they fail to comprehend that he is speaking

---

41. The pericope of the woman caught in adultery (7:53–8:11) is secondary and so has been excluded from consideration. See otherwise the indications of a consistent location and audience in 7:14, 28, 37–43; 8:12, 20. See finally "and he went out of the temple" in 8:59.

42. And so they ironically ask, "Where is your Father?" (8:19).

of his impending death. Instead, they ironically say, "Does he intend to kill himself?" (8:22). For they are from this world below (ἐκ τῶν κάτω). But he is from heaven above (ἐκ τῶν ἄνω). They are of this world. But he is not (8:23). Unless they comprehend these things, unless they hear of them from him, never will they see what they must see. And so Jesus says, "Unless you believe that I am [he] [ἐγώ εἰμι], you will die in your sins" (8:24).[43] But they are as uncertain of his meaning as ever. And so they ironically ask, "What do you mean? *Who are you?*"[44] Responding, he explicitly specifies what he was previously meaning to say. "[I am] what I have been telling you from the beginning," says Jesus (8:25). But they have not been hearing his words with ears that are ready to hear. Therefore, they do not see because they do not hear. He still has much to say that he has heard from the one who sent him. And the one who sent him is true (8:26). But, again (cf. 8:18), they do not understand that he is talking about his Father (8:27). In the end, they do not understand at all.

A time will come when what fails his followers now will do so no longer. So Jesus declares, "When you have lifted up the Son of Man, then you will know that I am [he] [ἐγώ εἰμι]"[45] (8:28; cf. 2:22; 12:16). Many hear in Jesus's words the promise of a better day. And they believe (8:30). But he knows that their sense of his words is inadequate. He knows that their believing will be short-lived. So Jesus urges them all to wait patiently on his promise of a day of greater clarity. And he says, "If you abide in my word, [the day will come when] you truly will be[46] my disciples. You will know the truth, and the truth will set you free" (8:31–32). Only those who

---

43. Cf. Jesus's recent statements that he is one from whom rivers of living water will soon flow (7:38; cf. 19:34), that he is, then, the anointed bearer and deliverer of the end-time Spirit of God (7:39; cf. those who therefore rightly conclude that he is then the Prophet and/or Christ of God in 7:40–41), that he is the Light of the World (8:12), and that he is God's Sent One (8:16), God's Witness (8:18), God's Son (8:19) from heaven above (8:23) who has come to do the end-time work of God. Recalling all this and more, he declares, "Unless you believe that I am [what I have been telling you] [cf. 8:25], you will die in your sins."

44. See the same question in 1:19; 21:12.

45. Then they will see what he has been telling them from the beginning (8:25). Cf. the references to a coming day of clarity in 2:22; 8:28; and 12:16. See further the lifting up of Jesus in 3:14 and 12:32–34, especially in 12:33: "He said this to show by what kind of death he was going to die."

46. Jesus says "if." "If" awaits the future. "If" awaits the resurrection (2:22; see also 8:28; 12:16). "If" suggests that ἐστέ is a futuristic present ("you will be").

see the day of his resurrection will be his true disciples. Only they will see. They will know the truth and will be free as is he.[47]

Sadly, his words offend once more. And so some say, "We have never been enslaved to anyone" (8:33). But Jesus speaks of a far greater enslavement than the one to which their thinking has turned (8:34). The slave to sin dwells not in God's house in the age that is to come (8:35). Only the one who is as Jesus is—only a son—dwells in God's house (cf. 1:12).[48] If thereby he sets them free, then will they be as he is (8:36). But this they do not see. Instead, because his word offends, they have tried to kill him (8:37). He speaks of what he alone has seen (8:38). But his Father is not their Father. Instead, they hear the word and do the works of their true father (8:41), the prince of darkness. If God were their Father, they would do what Abraham did (8:39). They would hear God's word of promise and believe. They would hear and love the One and Only One (1:18) who comes from God (8:42). But this they do not do. This they do not see. They do not see because they cannot stand the things they have heard. "Why do you not understand?" asks Jesus. "It is because you are unable to *hear my word*" (8:43).

Those who oppose Jesus are not of God. Instead, they are of their father, the devil (8:44). Their will is his will. His will is the will of a murderer. It has been this way from the beginning. They are the same, the hapless instruments of him who does not stand in the truth. In their father there is no truth. When he lies, he speaks out of his own character. For he is a liar. He is the father of lies. Jesus speaks the truth (8:45). Jesus is the Truth. But this they do not hear. They do not believe (8:45). They cannot believe (8:46). Like the One Who Is (ὁ ὤν, 1:18) himself,[49] every other "one who is [ὁ ὤν] of God hears God's words" (8:47). But they do not because they are not of God (8:46). They do not see the Truth. To see they must hear. To be of God they must hear. If they persist in their unwillingness to hear, they can never be of God. Jesus is uniquely of God. But all they see in Jesus is a despicable, demonic Samaritan (8:48).[50]

---

47. See further discussion to come.

48. "Son" refers, then, both to the sons and to the daughters of this world.

49. See further 3:31; 6:46; 12:12; Revelation 1:4, 8; 4:8; 11:17; 16:5.

50. Therefore, long before the exchange that follows, Jesus is in their minds more than worthy of death, insane or not. He blasphemes and is in their minds the most heinous of false prophets.

"Truly, truly, I say to you," adds Jesus, "if anyone heeds [τηρήσῃ][51] my word, by no means will he see death in the age that is to come" (8:51). But they take "see" (θεωρέω) to mean "taste" (γεύομαι) (8:52). They think that Jesus is speaking of the everyday experience of death. But Jesus's focus is the absence of this in the life of the age to come. For in him that age has come. He astounds them. So they ironically ask, "You are not [saying that you are] greater than our father Abraham, are you? Abraham died. All the prophets died [they all "tasted" death]. Who are you making yourself out to be?" (8:53). Jesus responds, saying, "You say of *my* Father, 'He is our God.' But you have not known him. I know him. And I heed his word" (8:54–55). To know the Father they must do likewise. They must heed the word of the Word Made Flesh.

"*Your* father Abraham rejoiced to see my day" (8:53a), adds Jesus. He looked to the future in faith and hope and prophetically "saw and was glad" (8:56b).[52] But, again, they fail to understand Jesus's words and take them to mean that Jesus is claiming to be old enough to have lived when Abraham lived[53]—a painfully ironic truth that is greater than they can possibly know. They take Jesus to be saying that he was when Abraham was. They take him to mean that, in Abraham's day, Abraham saw him, and he saw Abraham. So they say, "You are not yet fifty years old, and yet [how can you be saying that] you have seen Abraham?" (8:57).[54] Responding

---

51. The verb appears elsewhere in 2:10; 8:52, 55; 9:16; 12:7; 14:15, 21, 23, 24; 15:10, 20; 17:6, 11, 12, 15; 1 John 2:3, 4, 5; 3:22, 24; 5:3, 18. Its force is not narrow ("keeps" or "obeys") but is instead comprehensively broad ("heeds"; cf. the equivalents "attends to," "grasps," "embraces," "preserves," "retains," "hangs on to," "clings to," "cleaves to," "takes to heart," "treasures," "holds dear"). See further Bruce G. Schuchard, *1–3 John*, ConcC (Saint Louis: Concordia, 2012), 151–96.

52. "The first part of [Jesus'] statement is to be understood then as a general characterization of Abraham's significance as the receiver of God's promise. ... The expectation of fulfillment of that promise is then characterized by Jesus as a rejoicing." See Herman Ridderbos, *The Gospel of John: A Theological Commentary*, trans. John Vriend (Grand Rapids: Eerdmans, 1997), 320. Thus, "Abraham's joyful anticipation of the promise made to him and of its (provisional) fulfillment in the birth of Isaac is placed here in the perspective of the eschatological salvation that has dawned with the coming (the 'day') of Jesus" (321). What the Jews "now consistently reject in cynicism and unbelief Abraham long ago fervently longed for and 'saw' with 'rejoicing.' "

53. "The Jews understand Jesus to mean that he saw Abraham, that he was alive when Abraham was alive" (Thompson, *John*, 197).

54. "It is striking that—unlike Jesus in vs. 56—they speak of Jesus' seeing Abraham and not the reverse" (Ridderbos, *John*, 322).

directly to their mistaken understanding of his words,[55] Jesus astounds them again with even more than they are thinking that he has just said. He dumbfounds them, saying, "Truly, truly, I say to you. I am [he who was] before Abraham was" (8:58).[56] Reeling in horror in response to his words, they immediately take up stones to throw at him. But in keeping with the darkness that prevents them from seeing Jesus as he must be seen, he eludes them, concealing himself from them, and departs the temple (8:59).[57]

With very little suggestion of a narrative transition, what Jesus sees next is nothing new. Instead, what he encounters is emblematically more of the same. He and his disciples come across a man who cannot see (9:1). The man's malady comes from a father and a mother who are of this world. The man's circumstance is keenly suggestive of everything that is wrong with every living person. Symptomatically indicative of a condition that besets not some but all, the man is blind from birth. He has eyes, but they

---

55. It is precisely with their belief that Jesus has uttered an absurdity "that Jesus' answer connects" (Ridderbos, *John*, 322).

56. Thus, Jesus "claims to have existed before Abraham ever was," observes Marianne Meye Thompson, *John: A Commentary*, NTL (Louisville: Westminster John Knox, 2015), 197. See also Stanley E. Porter, *John, His Gospel, and Jesus: In Pursuit of the Johannine Voice* (Grand Rapids: Eerdmans, 2015), 139–40. What, however, Jesus does not say is when or how it was exactly that he ever preceded Abraham. They have asked, "You are not greater than our father Abraham, are you?" (8:53). His answer is, "I am! [ἐγὼ εἰμί]." See Ridderbos, *John*, 323. Cf. God's very similar manner of expressing himself in LXX Deuteronomy 32:39; Isaiah 41:4; 43:10, 25; 45:18, 19; 46:4; 51:12. See also Isaiah 45:8, 22; 46:9; 48:12, 17; 52:6. While Jesus's recurring manner of referring to himself with the words "I am [he]" (cf. 8:24, 28) bears a distinct relationship to the discourse of divine self-disclosure in the LXX and so should no doubt be read as decidedly freighted speech (cf., however, the man born blind in 9:9), never does the Johannine Jesus invoke God's name. Any attempt to suggest that he does so here or elsewhere must explain why in the synagogue of the first century and in the earliest church God's initial response to Moses' question "What is your name?" in Exodus 3:13 is not in LXX Exodus 3:14 ἐγὼ εἰμι ἐγὼ εἰμι (I am I AM) but is instead ἐγὼ εἰμι ὁ ὤν (I am the One Who Is), and why Moses is then instructed to tell Israel not that ἐγὼ εἰμι ἀπέσταλκέν με (I AM has sent me) but that ὁ ὤν ἀπέσταλκέν με (The One Who Is has sent me). See further the actual giving of God's name in MT Exodus 3:15, where God says to Moses, "Say this to the people of Israel, 'Yahweh, the God of your fathers, the God of Abraham, the God of Isaac, and the God of Jacob, has sent me to you.' *This is my name* forever, and thus I am to be remembered throughout all generations." Similarly, see Richard Bauckham, *Who Is God? Key Moments of Biblical Revelation*, ASBT (Grand Rapids: Baker Academic, 2020), 35–45. In the rest of the Hebrew Bible the name Yahweh appears more than 6,800 times. Never does אֶהְיֶה ("I am" or, more likely, "I will be") in the Hebrew of 3:14 (see elsewhere in the Pentateuch the use of the form only in Exod 3:12; 4:12, 15, to Moses and in Deut 31:23 to Joshua) or ὁ ὤν in the Greek appear elsewhere either in the MT or in the LXX as the name of God. See also the treatment of μονογενὴς θεὸς ὁ ὤν in 1:18. See further the excursus on the ἐγὼ εἰμι sayings of Jesus in John in Thompson, *John*, 156–60.

57. Cf. the references to the temple with no intervening indication of a change in Jesus's location in 7:14, 28, 37; 8:20.

do not see. The Light of the World (8:12) has come so that those without sight might see (9:39). He has come so the darkness would be no more. The Light gives light. The Light gives sight. He does so when he speaks.

The disciples ask after a cause for the man's blindness. They ask why (9:2). Jesus directs their attention elsewhere. The man is blind, suggests Jesus, and is before them so the works of God may be manifest (9:3).[58] The man is blind so he may embody what Jesus has come to be and to do.[59] While the Light of the World is present, it is day (9:4a). While it is day, Jesus must work the works of the one who sent him to do God's work. When his work is done (cf. "It is finished" in 19:30), the Light of the World will rest in the grave. Night (νύξ) will come. And none will see. When Jesus rests, no subsequent work will need to be done (9:4b). For the work to be done will be at an end. In anticipation of its end, Jesus says, "As long as I am in the world, I am the Light of the World" (9:5). As long as he is in the world, the Light gives light. The Light gives sight (1:9). He gives sight when the Word Made Flesh says and does what he has come to do.[60]

Jesus spits[61] on the ground[62] and mixes the spittle[63] of his mouth with the dust of the ground. And Jesus anoints[64] the blind man's unseeing eyes with the transforming, life- and light-giving mix[65] of the two (9:6).[66] And the Sent One sends a newly sent one to wash in the pool whose very name—Siloam—means "sent." For when heaven benevolently sends, and

---

58. The main clause that ἀλλ' in 9:3 followed by ἵνα assumes likely implies not that "this has happened so that" but that "this circumstance presents itself so that." See further the combination of the two in 1:8, 31; 3:17; 11:52; 12:9, 47; 13:18; 14:31; 15:25; 17:15.

59. See Köstenberger, *John*, 277.

60. Cf. the expectation that Messiah would be a "light to the nations" and "open the eyes of the blind" in Isaiah 42:6–7; 51:4.

61. The vocable πτύω (spit) appears elsewhere in the Greek of the LXX and New Testament only in Num 12:14 and in Mark 7:33; 8:23.

62. The vocable χαμαι (on the ground) appears elsewhere in the New Testament only in 18:6.

63. The vocable πτύσμα (spittle) appears nowhere else in the Greek of the LXX and New Testament.

64. The vocable ἐπιχρίω (anoint) appears only here and in 9:11 in the Greek of the LXX and New Testament.

65. See further πηλός (mud/clay) in 9:11, 14, 15; and the Creator's fashioning of man from the same in LXX Isaiah 29:16; 45:9; 64:7; Jeremiah 18:6; and Romans 9:21. See also LXX Job 4:19; 10:9; 30:19; 33:6; 38:14; and Sirach 33:13.

66. Cf. the Creator's fashioning of Adam from the ground out of which "a fountain rose and watered the whole face of the earth" in LXX Genesis 2:6–7.

sent ones do what they are sent to do, supremely good things happen.[67]
The sightless one complies with the word of the Word Made Flesh (cf.
4:50). He goes and he washes and, when he has washed, he sees (9:7).
He sees but does not see.[68]

Later, those previously acquainted with the man are astonished to see
that he now sees. Others refuse to believe what they are now hearing. They
attempt instead to suggest that the now-seeing one is only pretending to be
the previously not-seeing one. To this, the seeing one poignantly declares,
"I am [he]" (ἐγώ εἰμι, 9:9).[69] He knows who he himself is. He knows, at
least in part, who his healer is.[70] He recalls what he has heard. He has
heard and therefore knows his healer's name. It was the one named Jesus
who gave him sight. So the man knows who. And the man knows how
(9:11). There is much that he therefore knows. But what he shows that
he otherwise does not yet know is precisely what he must know if he is
to see Jesus as Jesus must be seen. He knows that Jesus gave him sight on
the Sabbath (9:14).[71] But he does not now know where Jesus is (9:12).[72]

---

67. Cf. Elisha who sends Naaman to wash in the Jordan in 2 Kings 5:10–13. John 9 is the only
New Testament text that mentions the pool of Siloam. Cf. the tower in Luke 13:4. The source of the
ritual water for the Feast of Tabernacles in John 7 was the pool of Siloam.

68. "The pool is located elsewhere in Jerusalem. The man cannot see. All he has is the directive
to go and wash—and Jesus does not even explain *why* he should grope his way across town to the
pool instead of wiping the mud off his eyes at the place where he was sitting. Yet Jesus's words evoke
a willingness to trust. The man goes as Jesus tells him to do, even though he has not yet experienced
healing. After washing, the man discovers that he can see. His initial trust in Jesus seems well placed.
The man sees—*but he does not see Jesus.*" See Koester, *Word of Life*, 167. There is even more than this
to what the now seeing one does not see.

69. The beggar's apparently everyday use here of the expression ἐγώ εἰμι serves significantly
to explain why elsewhere the use of the same expression by Jesus regularly meets with little to no
reaction on the part of his hearers. The expression bears no inherent freight in and of itself. When
the phrase does or does not bear the freight of divine self-disclosure can then only be determined
from context. Thus, how the persistently enigmatic Jesus is to be heard is never quite clear to any
who hear him until he is risen from the dead (2:22; see also 8:28; 12:16).

70. Contrast the healed one in 5:12–13.

71. For the possible ways in which Jesus may thus have transgressed the law of the Pharisees,
see Köstenberger, *John*, 285–86.

72. See further what he and the others know or do not know in 9:20, 21, 24, 25, 29, 30, 31.
Conspicuously, his interlocutors fail to know because they refuse to hear (9:27). Ironically, they question him "about a Jesus whom he has never seen," notes Craig R. Koester, "Jesus' Resurrection, the
Signs, and the Dynamics of Faith," in *The Resurrection of Jesus in the Gospel of John*, ed. Craig R. Koester
and Reimund Bieringer, WUNT 222 (Tubingen: Mohr Siebeck, 2008), 63. If hearing, they too would
become disciples of him whom God hears (9:31). Contrast their scornful response to the beggar's
comments in defense of Jesus: "and you are teaching us?" (9:34). See further Köstenberger, *John*, 291–93.

The man takes Jesus to be "a/the prophet" (9:17; cf. 4:19).[73] But he does not know whether Jesus is or is not a sinner (9:25). The man knows that "if this [Jesus] were not from God, he could do nothing" (9:33). But when Jesus returns to him at a later time to ask him, "Do you believe in the Son of Man?" (9:35), the man responds with "Who is he, sir [κύριε], [tell me] so that I may believe" (9:36).

For the first time, the man sees Jesus. But there is more that Jesus must do. Seeing does not suffice. The man sees but does not see. He sees but does not yet know who Jesus is. But what he *trusts* is that the one with whom he is speaking does. What the man poignantly expresses a willingness to believe is *whatever Jesus says*. What he emblematically says he is ready to hear is the word of the Word Made Flesh. "Tell me," says the man, "and I will believe what you tell me." "You have seen him," replies Jesus, "and the one who is speaking with you [now] is he" (9:37). Only then, in response to the solely sufficient explicit word of the Word Made Flesh, does the blind man see.[74] And he venerates Jesus (9:38).[75] Jesus marks the definitive nature of what has transpired, saying, "For judgment I came into this world, so that those who do not see may see, and so those who see may become blind" (9:39). Some of the Pharisees who are near hear this and say, "Are we also blind?" (9:40). "If you were blind," replies Jesus, "[that is to say, if you looked to me and to my word so that you might see] you would have no sin." But because they cannot bear to hear his word and instead presume to say "We see [already what we need to see]," their sin remains (9:41).[76]

With no suggestion of a change in location or audience,[77] Jesus continues to speak of his unseen person and purpose. To those who are seeing

---

73. The predicate nominative precedes the copula in the Greek and so may be construed as definite ("the prophet") rather than indefinite ("a prophet"). Cf. the Samaritan woman in 4:19. See further 7:40. Thus, the healed one speaks again a truth that is greater than he knows.

74. Similarly, see Deborah Forger, "Jesus as God's Word(s): Aurality, Epistemology, and Embodiment in the Gospel of John," *JSNT* 42 (2020): 285.

75. The all too usual translation "and he worshiped [προσεκύνησεν] him" is exceedingly misleading. See BDAG, s.v. προσκυνέω. None know yet that Jesus is worthy of worship. Yet the man's actions ironically express again a truth that is greater than he knows.

76. "The authorities have the illusion that they can see the truth. They are blind to their own blindness" (Koester, *Word of Life*, 73). Jesus therefore calls them "blind guides" in Matthew 15:14; 23:16, 24. See also 23:17, 19, 26.

77. See Ridderbos, *John*, 352–53.

but not seeing, he says, "Truly, truly, I say to you. The one who does not enter into the dwelling place [εἰς τὴν αὐλήν][78] of the sheep by the door [διὰ τῆς θύρας][79] but ascends by another way, that one is a thief [κλέπτης][80] and a robber [λῃστής].[81] But the one who enters by the door is the shepherd [ποιμήν] of the sheep. For this one the gatekeeper [θυρωρός][82] opens. The sheep hear his voice. And he calls his own [τὰ ἴδια][83] sheep [πρόβατα] by name[84] and leads them out. When he has brought out all those who are his own [ἴδια],[85] he goes before them. And the sheep follow him. For they know his voice. A stranger they will by no means follow. Instead, they will flee from him. For they do not know the voice of strangers" (10:1–5). Jesus shares this foreshadowing illustrative figure (παροιμία)[86] with them. But as before so also here, none of them comprehend his words (10:6).

By means of a second illustrative figure linked to the first but not to be confused with it, Jesus says more. He seeks again to inform what his person and work will mean to the one who finally sees. He says, "Truly, truly, I say to you, I am the Door [θύρα] of the sheep. All who came before me are thieves and robbers. But the sheep did not listen to them. I am the Door. If anyone enters by me [δι' ἐμοῦ], he will be saved [σωθήσεται]. He will go in and come out. And he will find pasture [νομήν]" (10:7–9).[87] All, then, will be as it should be. All will be secure. All will be fed.[88]

Jesus's two illustrative figures (10:1–6, 7–10) describe a necessary sequence. First, the Good Shepherd must enter. He must enter by the

---

78. An αὐλή is an enclosed open space, a courtyard, or is by extension an entire dwelling place. See BDAG, s.v. αὐλή. Cf. the sheep that are not of the αὐλή of which Jesus speaks in 10:16; the αὐλή of the high priest in 18:15; and the αὐλή of the temple in Revelation 11:2.

79. See further the vocable θύρα (door) in 10:2, 7, 9; 18:16; 20:19, 26; Revelation 3:8, 20; 4:1.

80. Cf. Judas in 12:6.

81. Cf. Barabbas in 18:40.

82. Cf. θυρωρός (gatekeeper) in 18:16–17.

83. Contrast "he came to his own [εἰς τὰ ἴδια], but his own [οἱ ἴδιοι] received him not" in 1:11.

84. See further discussion on Lazarus in 11:43 and Mary in 20:16.

85. Cf. ἐκβάλλω (drive out) in 2:15.

86. See further παροιμία (illustrative figure) in 16:25, 29.

87. "Pasture" (νομή) appears elsewhere in the New Testament only in 2 Timothy 2:17. Cf. Psalm 73:1; 78:13; 94:7; 99:3.

88. They go out. They do not return. See D. A. Carson, *The Gospel according to John*, PNTC (Grand Rapids: Eerdmans, 1991), 383. True security is now to be found in the company of the Good Shepherd. True food is what he alone provides.

door. Only then will the Shepherd become the Door. Only then will the one who enters and comes back out by the Door that is Jesus live.[89] Only then will the one who dies and rises with Jesus who is first to traverse the way be saved. Only this one will find pasture (10:9). "I am the Good Shepherd," declares Jesus. The Good Shepherd alone does what no other shepherd would do (10:12–13). The Good Shepherd enters by the door (see further below 18:15–16). He thus "lays down his life [ψυχήν] for the sheep" (10:11). He knows his own. And his own know him (10:14).[90] So Jesus says it again: "I lay down my life [ψυχήν] for the sheep" (10:15).

There are other sheep. They are not of Israel. They are not of the dwelling place (αὐλή) of the people of God (10:16a; cf. "salvation is of the Jews," 4:22).[91] They too will hear the voice of the Word Made Flesh. They too will come. Then there will be "one flock [ποίμνη]"[92] and "one shepherd [ποιμήν]" (10:16b; cf. 1:11–12).[93] Therefore, for the third time Jesus says it. And the third time he says it three times. He will lay down his life (ψυχήν) for them all (10:17–18).[94] Again, his hearers are divided *on account of his words* (10:19). Some say, "He has a demon and is out of his mind. Why are you listening to him?" (10:20). But others protest, saying, "These are not the words of a demoniac. A demon cannot open the eyes of the blind, can he?" (10:21). What divides and defines them is once more the word of the Word Made Flesh.

At the Feast of the Dedication (ἐγκαίνια),[95] still in Jerusalem (10:22), those weary of Jesus find him again. In the temple, in the colonnade of

---

89. "The righteous enter into salvation through the 'gate of the Lord.' " Thompson, *John*, 223. See LXX Psalm 117:19–20. Cf. Revelation 3:8; 4:1.

90. See "good" (καλός) in 10:11, 14, 32, 33; and 2:10. Cf. the seven times that the adjective appears in LXX Genesis 1:1–25 followed by "very good" in 1:31.

91. The αὐλή of the sheep (10:1) is "the whole of historic Israel" (Ridderbos, *John*, 363). "Other sheep" refers to the gentiles. See Köstenberger, *John*, 306n45.

92. "Flock" (ποίμνη) appears elsewhere in the Greek of the LXX and New Testament only in Genesis 32:17; Matthew 26:31; Luke 2:8; 1 Corinthians 9:7.

93. See Ezek 34:23. "The notion of one flock being led by one shepherd as a metaphor for God's providential care for his united people is firmly rooted in OT prophetic literature and continued in later Jewish writings" (Köstenberger, *John*, 307). See further Köstenberger.

94. Cf. ψυχή in 10:24–27; 13:37–38; 15:13. Jesus lays down his life so that the sons and daughters of Adam may themselves have life. Cf. Adam, who becomes a living ψυχή in LXX Genesis 2:7.

95. This is the only New Testament text that refers to the Feast of the Dedication. See further the feast in Köstenberger, *John*, 309, who deems it possible that Jesus spent the two months from Tabernacles in John 7 to Dedication in John 10 in Jerusalem.

Solomon (10:23), they challenge him, saying, "How long will you hold us in suspense? If you are the Christ,[96] tell us openly [παρρησίᾳ]" (10:24; cf. 7:4). Jesus responds, saying, "I did tell you. But you do not believe" (10:25). By his word, by the rest of his deeds as well—by all such "works" (ἔργα)—Jesus has already addressed the question of who he is and why he has come (10:25). But they are not sheep of the Shepherd (10:26) who always hear his voice (10:3–5). If they were, they would hear him. If they were, they would believe him. But they do not.

"I and the Father," adds Jesus, "we are one [ἕν]" (10:30).[97] Again, his words offend. Again, they take up stones to throw at him (10:31). "I have shown you many good works from the Father. For which of them are you going to stone me?" asks Jesus (10:32). There is much that he has done. But his words have offended the most. So they say, "We are not taking up stones to throw at you for a good work but for blasphemy. Though you are [no more than] a man [ἄνθρωπος ὤν], you speak and act as if you were God!"[98] (10:33). The ironic truth that they speak is so much greater than they can possibly know. Jesus responds with Scripture. He responds with a psalm because he knows that the psalm's remarkable words are well suited to the nature of their charge. He knows that Psalm 82:6 (LXX 81:6) refers to "sons of the Most High" who have responsibility for the governance of God's people as "gods."[99] So he asks them, "Is it

---

96. Cf. "Son of God" in 10:36.

97. Cf. "that they may be one [ἕν] even as we are one [ἕν]" in 17:21–22. See further Köstenberger, *John*, 312.

98. In their minds, "you make yourself to be God" (ποιεῖς σεαυτὸν θεόν, 10:33) means not "you claim to be God" (a possibility that they never would have considered) but "you handle yourself and thus speak as if you were God." Cf. Carson, *John*, 396, who notes the irony of their words, for Jesus is not he who makes himself God but he who makes himself man (1:14). "Blasphemy" (βλασφημία) appears only here in the Gospel. Cf. the singular use of the verb βλασφημέω in 10:36.

99. For the various positions that have been taken regarding the psalm's addressees, see Köstenberger, *John*, 315. That they are unjust Israelite rulers is suggested (1) when the psalmist states in LXX Psalm 81 that "God stands in the assembly [ἐν συναγωγῇ] of the gods and in the midst of them he judges gods" in 81:1 (God is the defender of justice; those who uphold justice as his ruling representatives in this world do so *in his stead* and by his command); (2) when God as judge indicts them for being unjust judges in 81:2; (3) when God summons them to just judgments and to the care of the poor and the needy in 81:3–4; (4) when God says that the gods "know not and do not understand" and that they "walk on in darkness" in 81:5; (5) when God acknowledges that he himself has likened their person and purpose to his (cf. Exod 4:16; 7:1; theirs is a purpose analogous to his own in that they are agents of justice, his justice) and calls them "gods" and "sons of the Most High" in 81:6; (6) when God says that, in spite of the greatness to which God has elevated them, as (mere mortal?) men they will die and as (deserving unjust?) rulers they will fall in 81:7; (7) when

not written in your [own] law, 'I said, you are gods?' " (10:34). With this he then mounts an argument in defense of himself. He argues that if their own Scripture calls[100] them gods to whom the word of God previously came (10:35a),[101] then Scripture supports not them but him. Scripture (ἡ γραφή) cannot be broken (10:35b). It is irrefutable. How then can the Word Made Flesh whom the Father set apart[102] and sent[103] be guilty of blasphemy for saying what he has said? How can the Speech of the God who speaks be wrong in saying, "I am the Son of God"?[104] (10:35–36; cf. "the Christ" in 10:24). He is not.

The ingenuity of the Word Made Flesh leaves them with no words of their own with which to respond. To be sure, Jesus knows that his word is once more far more than they can bear (cf. 6:60; 8:43). So he exhorts his interlocutors to find in the rest of his works reason to believe that "the Father is in me and I am in the Father" (10:37–38).[105] Sadly, his words offend once more. And they seek to arrest him. But he escapes their grasp

---

(completing a frame for the psalm; cf. 81:1) the psalmist expresses his longing for the day when God will come as Judge of all the nations and says, "Arise, O God, judge the earth" in 81:8; and (8) when Jesus describes the "gods" as those "to whom the word of God came" in John 10:35. Jesus's use of the psalm with what follows makes sense only if the psalm's gods are unjust Israelite rulers. Cf. those with whom Jesus is speaking!

100. Köstenberger, *John*, 314n81, argues persuasively that the understood subject of εἶπεν (calls) in 10:35 is not God but is instead the law to which Jesus has just referred. The result is an informing continuity of subjects in 10:34–35.

101. Köstenberger, *John*, 314–15, observes rightly that in Old Testament Scripture, those to whom "the word of the Lord came" are very often "those who speak or act in God's name." See the Baptist in Luke 3:2.

102. "Set apart" (ἁγιάζω) appears in the Gospel only here and in 17:17, 19.

103. To be "set apart and sent" is to come as the agent of the sender in the full authority of the sender. Both Sender and Sent One are one.

104. Again, the predicate nominative (υἱός) precedes the copula (εἰμί) in the Greek and so may be (yet also need not be) construed as definite ("the Son") rather than indefinite ("a son"). Here, "Son of God" recalls their initial challenge: "If you are the Christ, tell us openly" (10:24). For he is God's Son, meaning, "Messiah, king of Israel" (1:49). And their complaint is not that he has claimed to be God, but that he as Son has claimed that Father and Son are one.

105. In response to those who are "deaf to his words, Jesus here makes a final appeal to the undeniable character of his many 'good' deeds" (Ridderbos, *John*, 372). For they too are works that testify. See 5:36; 10:25; 14:10–11.

(10:39) and returns to the place beyond the Jordan where John first was (see Bethany in 1:28). There Jesus remains (10:40). There many come to Jesus, saying, "John did no sign, but everything that John said about this man was true." And many believe in him there (10:41–42).

For the third and last time the testimony of John marks the conclusion to the last of Jesus's three trips in the Gospel's first half to Jerusalem (1:19–10:42). The Gospel's first half ends in the same place and in the same way that its story of Jesus began. It ends with Jesus, with the speaking of John, and with many believing.[106] In the Gospel's first half, essential, solely sufficient testimony is given that later must inform the arrival and the accomplishment of his hour. Later the word of the Word Made Flesh must inform his person and work if any are to see Jesus as finally he must be seen.

---

106. Cf. Carson, *John*, 147, who similarly observes that the public ministry of Jesus "begins and ends at Bethany" (1:28). Alternatively, Bauckham, *Gospel of Glory*, 138, suggests that the Gospel's first week (1:19–2:11) and its passion week both begin with a Bethany (see 1:28; 11:1,18; 12:1). According to Bauckham, "The place name signals that we are to look for further parallels between the two weeks."

CHAPTER FIVE

A TROUBLED THOMAS *and* *a* DEAD MAN RISES

John 11:1–57

In the story of Jesus that follows (11:1–57), the Gospel's second half (11:1–20:31) begins in the same way that it ends.[1] It begins with a troubled Thomas and with a dead man who rises.[2] For the first time, the narrative mentions Thomas. For the first time, Thomas speaks not only for himself but also for the rest of his fellow disciples. They are all alarmed that Jesus is determined to return to Judea. And yet they go with him. In Bethany, Lazarus is dead. And his sisters, Mary and Martha, are mourning the loss of their brother. Jesus instructs them to remove the stone that is covering the mouth of the tomb. In their hearing, Jesus prays to his Father. He prays so they too would hear and see what they are failing to see. With a loud voice, Jesus cries out, saying, "Lazarus, come out!" Jesus calls Lazarus by name. As all must do, the dead man heeds the voice of the Shepherd. He heeds the word of the Word Made Flesh and is freed from the bandages of death.

The story of Jesus that follows begins also with a first reference to Lazarus and his sisters (11:1–2). Lazarus is ill. So his sisters, Mary and

---

1. See Andreas Köstenberger, *John*, BECNT (Grand Rapids: Baker Academic, 2004), 322, who argues that the raising of Lazarus in John 11 anticipates the resurrection of Jesus in John 20.

2. At the end, however, the order of the two is reversed. The resulting *a b b a* pattern serves nicely as a frame for the second half. Cf. above the analysis of 1:19–10:42.

Martha, send for Jesus, saying, "He whom you love is ill" (11:3). At a distance, and already days later,[3] Jesus responds. As before (cf. 9:3), Jesus sees the circumstance of Lazarus and his sisters as an opportunity for the followers of Jesus to see his glory (11:4).[4] The circumstance exists so they may see again what Jesus has come to be and to do. Jesus has come for those he loves. Jesus loves Lazarus and his sisters (11:5). Yet Jesus strangely waits for two more days (11:6).[5] *He waits for Lazarus to die.*[6] Only then is Jesus ready to go. Only then does he say to his disciples, "Let us go to Judea again" (11:7).

The disciples react with understandable alarm (11:8). In Judea, those opposing Jesus will no doubt attempt again to kill him. Aware of their trepidation, Jesus affirms that, as long as the Light of the World is with them, it is day and is no time for stumbling (11:9–10). It is instead time for Jesus's work to be done (cf. 9:4–5). And so Jesus declares, "Lazarus sleeps [κεκοίμηται]. But I go to awaken him" (11:11).[7] Again, they fail to comprehend the word of the Word Made Flesh (11:12–13). Again, they ironically speak a truth that is greater than they can possibly know, saying, "Lord, if he sleeps, σωθήσεται" (11:12).[8] From their unwitting vantage point they are thinking that Lazarus will recover/awaken. The greater truth is that Lazarus will be saved (cf. 10:9).

Jesus makes plain his meaning, saying, "Lazarus has died" (11:14). Again, he suggests that the resulting circumstance exists so they may see and believe (11:15; cf. 11:4). Despite their misgivings, he says once more, "Let us go." His disciples are totally bewildered by the apparent death wish of their master. Despairing of what seems inevitable given the

---

3. Later, it takes four days for Jesus and his disciples to make their way to Bethany (see further below). It likely took a similar amount of time for the message of the sisters to get to Jesus.

4. See D. A. Carson, *The Gospel according to John*, PNTC (Grand Rapids: Eerdmans, 1991), 406.

5. Köstenberger, *John*, 328, observes, "On the face of it, this is a classic non sequitur. One would have expected Jesus to rush to the scene instantaneously. Yet once again the evangelist confounds conventional thinking in his presentation." What Jesus has in mind can only happen if he waits for Lazarus to die.

6. "Apparently, Lazarus was still alive when the initial news regarding his illness reached Jesus," observes Köstenberger, *John*, 328. "Two days later, Jesus, presumably by means of supernatural insight, announces to his followers that Lazarus has died." Only then do they depart.

7. For such sleep, see further Köstenberger, *John*, 330–31.

8. For the irony of what follows, see Francis J. Moloney, *John*, SP 4 (Collegeville, MN: Liturgical Press, 1998), 326–27.

determination of Jesus to return to the stronghold of those who oppose him, one of them speaks again for all of them.[9] Thomas, known also as Didymus (see also 20:24; 21:2),[10] speaks not only for himself but also for the rest of his "fellow disciples" (συμμαθηταί).[11] What lies ahead for them all seems certain. And so Thomas says, "Let us also go so that *we* [too] may die with him" (11:16).[12]

Days later, Martha, the older of the two sisters,[13] hears that Jesus is soon to arrive (11:20). But her brother is dead. And his corpse has been in the grave for four days (11:17).[14] Rigor mortis has set in. The body is in a state of decay (see 11:39). Martha goes out to greet Jesus. But Mary remains in the house (11:20). If only Jesus had come sooner, her brother could have been saved (11:21).[15] But this many days later the time for the

---

9. Similarly, see Nicodemus in 3:2; the Samaritan woman in 4:12, 17–18, 20; and Peter in 6:68–69. That Thomas expresses the later bravado of Peter (13:37) is unlikely given the Gospel's characterization of Thomas here and below.

10. To translate here or elsewhere with "Thomas, called *the Twin*" is at best misleading. More likely it is mistaken. *Both* the disciple's Jewish name "Thomas" and his Greek name "Didymus" are proper names meaning "twin." See BDAG, s.v. Θωμᾶς and Δίδυμος. Cf. the proper names "Cephas" and "Peter" in 1:42, both names meaning "rock." Therefore, "Twin" is not for Thomas a nickname (or the like) unrelated to the name that his parents gave him. "Twin" is what his name means both in their native tongue and culture and in Hellenism.

11. See especially "us" and "we" with what follows. See further "we" twice in 14:5. Thus, consistent with this disciple's two names that both mean "twin," the New Testament *hapax legomenon* "fellow disciple" (συμμαθητής) suggests further that here and elsewhere Thomas speaks in a representative capacity. The evaluative point of view from which he speaks is that of the rest of his "fellow disciples." See Köstenberger, *John*, 332, citing Leon Morris, *The Gospel according to John*, rev. ed., NICNT (Grand Rapids: Eerdmans, 1995), 483. He is just like the rest of them, and they are just like him.

12. That what Thomas declares sounds "like fatalistic resignation to what seemed inevitable" is suggested by Ben Witherington III in *John's Wisdom: A Commentary on the Fourth Gospel* (Louisville: Westminster John Knox, 1995), 202. Köstenberger agrees, noting the range of alternatives that have been considered by others (*John*, 332n48). Again, the truth that this follower of Jesus speaks is greater than he knows. He and his fellow disciples will all die at a later time for the sake of Jesus. But they will do so for reasons that Thomas and the rest of his fellow disciples are presently failing to see.

13. See Ridderbos, *John*, 404.

14. The hearer is not told where in 11:1–16 Jesus was. Johannes Beutler notes the day is now a *sixth day*, and finds this fitting, given the six-day-long weeks with which the Gospel begins and ends. Beutler, *A Commentary on the Gospel of John*, trans. Michael Tait (Grand Rapids: Eerdmans, 2017), 8. Thus, Jesus receives the message of the sisters on day one (11:4), remains for two more days (11:6), departs on the day of the death and burial of Lazarus (11:7–15), which is day three, and arrives in Bethany when Lazarus has already been in the grave for four days (11:17), which is day six, the reverse of what was observed above regarding the numbering of the days in 1:19–2:1. That it was "customary for burial in ancient Palestine to take place on the day of death" is noted by Köstenberger, *John*, 333.

15. By now the sisters have been hoping for Jesus to arrive for more than a week! For the suggestion that Martha's initial manner of greeting Jesus betrays "a hint of disappointment at Jesus'

hope of such things is, from the perspective of Martha, now long since past. It is too late for their brother, at least as regards the *now*.[16] But what of the *not yet*? What of the resurrection that is to come?

The experience of their brother's death has shaken his sisters. Yet Martha does not waver in her understanding of Jesus. Instead, rather remarkably, she poignantly persists in her confident belief that Jesus is Israel's Messiah. That he has come too late for her brother changes nothing.[17] What ultimately matters is not the present but the future, not what is but what will be. Therefore, Martha resolutely declares, "Even now I know that, whatever you ask from God, God will give you" (11:22).[18] Extraordinarily, she continues to believe that Jesus is what they have taken him to be. Through Jesus the glorious future that Israel awaits will most certainly come. When it comes, her brother will rise. All the dead will rise.

"Your brother will rise," declares Jesus (11:23). Jesus is thinking of the *now* and the *not yet*. But Martha thinks that Jesus is speaking only of the day when all the dead will rise (see 5:28–29).[19] So Martha replies, saying, "Yes, Lord. I know that he will rise in the resurrection on the last day" (11:24). She has been listening (see also 5:25–27; 6:39–40, 44, 54).[20] Therefore, Martha expresses her tremendous and abiding hope that her brother will rise when the rest of the dead rise. But what she does not yet know and so does not now expect is that her brother will rise sooner than she thinks. "I am the Resurrection and the Life" (11:25), declares Jesus. He means to be this for her brother not later but now. "Do you believe

---

delay" see Köstenberger, *John*, 334. See also Herman Ridderbos, *The Gospel of John: A Theological Commentary*, trans. John Vriend (Grand Rapids: Eerdmans, 1997), 395.

16. "Later Jewish sources attest the rabbinic belief that death was irrevocable three days after a person had died," observes Köstenberger, *John*, 333. See Lev. Rab. 18.1. Cf. Eccles. Rab. 12.6. See also m. Yebam. 16.3; Sem. 8, rule 1.

17. "Martha not only believes without seeing, she believes in spite of what she sees," notes Craig R. Koester, "Jesus' Resurrection, the Signs, and the Dynamics of Faith," in *The Resurrection of Jesus in the Gospel of John*, ed. Craig R. Koester and Reimund Bieringer, WUNT 222 (Tubingen: Mohr Siebeck, 2008), 64.

18. On the one hand, she speaks again a truth that is greater than she knows. At the same time, she shows that she does not yet know who Jesus really is. Cf. "you ask *God*" and "*God* will give to you." Jesus need not ask of God (5:22–30). She needs to ask of him.

19. See Craig R. Koester, *Symbolism in the Fourth Gospel: Meaning, Mystery, Community*, 2nd ed. (Minneapolis: Fortress, 2003), 168.

20. See further the (frequently untranslated) word of Jesus regarding "the age that is to come" in 4:14; 6:51, 58; 8:35, 51–52; 9:32; 10:28; 11:26.

this?" asks Jesus (11:26). Martha's response is both marvelously witting and unwitting. As much as she is thus far able, she takes the word of the Word Made Flesh to heart and believes it. And she speaks a truth that is profoundly greater than she can possibly know when she says, "Yes, Lord, I believe that you are the Christ, the Son of God, the Coming One" (11:27; cf. 1:9).[21]

Then Martha goes to her sister. And Martha tells Mary that the Teacher is calling for her (11:28). When Mary hears this, she goes quickly to Jesus (11:29). And Mary repeats what Martha has already said (11:21). "Lord," says Mary, "if you had been here, my brother would not have died" (11:32). In other words, Mary shows that her understanding of the moment is the same as that of her sister. Their brother is dead and gone. His body awaits the resurrection, as do they. Her grief, her sense of loss, is great. A better day seems far away. So she and others with her weep and wail.[22] When Jesus sees this, he is deeply aggravated in his spirit and greatly troubled (ἐνεβριμήσατο τῷ πνεύματι καὶ ἐτάραξεν ἑαυτόν, 11:33).[23] And he says, "Where have you laid him?" They respond, saying, "Lord, come and see" (11:34). But the moment is no time for *him* to come and see. The moment is a time for *them* to come and see (see 1:39, 46; 4:29). Neither is it a time for weeping. So Jesus also weeps (11:35).[24] But he does so not out of sympathy for them (11:36). Rather, Jesus weeps on account of their deeply distressing inability even now to see who he is and what it is that he has come to be and to do.[25] Only he sees. Only he knows what soon

---

21. "Like Nathanael in 1:49, Martha apparently used the title 'Son of God' in a traditional messianic sense without understanding its full import" (Koester, *Symbolism*, 121). Köstenberger, *John*, 336, adds her confession "strikingly anticipates the purpose statement at the end of the Gospel." The result is yet another *inclusio* in support of the others that help to frame the Gospel's second half. Morris, *John*, 489, observes, "She may not understand fully the implications of what he has just said, but as far as she can she accepts it."

22. "According to Jewish funeral custom, even a poor family was expected to hire at least two flute players and a wailing woman (m. Ketub. 4.4), and Mary and Martha's family appears to have been anything but poor" (Köstenberger, *John*, 338). See further on the analysis of 12:1–3.

23. For the "bewildering array of interpretations" that scholars have produced in response to this verse's language, see Köstenberger, *John*, 338–42. Jesus is visibly agitated. He bristles, is stirred, is in anguish, and is full of indignation in response to what he sees. He is angry. Cf. the use of ταράσσω in 12:27; 13:21. Contrast "let not your hearts be troubled" in 14:1, 27.

24. "Weep" (δακρύω) appears only here in the New Testament. Cf. LXX Job 3:24.

25. Likewise, Moloney, *John*, 331.

will be. When the time comes for Jesus to go to the cross, only he will go. And he will go alone (16:32).[26] And so Jesus weeps.

Some of them say, "Was this one who opened the eyes of the blind man unable to act so that this [other] one would not have died?" (11:37). Aggravated all the more by their incomprehension, Jesus instructs them to remove the stone from the mouth of the tomb (11:38–39). Once more, Martha unwittingly responds, saying, "Lord, it [by now the body] already reeks [with the stench of death], for it is the fourth day" (11:39). But Jesus responds, saying, "Did I not tell you that *if you believe you will see* the glory of God?" (11:40).[27] Then they will see what fails them now. At his word, they take away the stone that is covering the mouth of the tomb. And Jesus prays in their hearing to his Father who always hears Jesus. Jesus does this so they too would hear now and then later see what they have failed to see (11:41–42).[28] With a loud voice he cries out,[29] saying, "Lazarus, come out!" He calls Lazarus *by name* (11:43; cf. 10:3; see also 5:28–29).[30] The dead man (τεθνηκώς)[31] heeds the great voice (φωνή μεγάλη)[32] of the Good Shepherd. As all must do, he heeds the word of the Word Made Flesh and is freed (8:31–32, 36) from the bandages of death (11:44).[33]

Many who see this believe (11:45). But others report it to the Pharisees (11:46). The Pharisees fear with the priests and the rest of the Sanhedrin

---

26. Cf. his cry of dereliction in Matthew 27:46; Mark 15:34.

27. Contrast seeing in order to believe (4:48; 6:30) with believing in order to see (here). Cf. believing in order to know in 6:69. See further on the analysis of "unless I see ... I will by no means believe" in 20:25; and of "have you believed because you have seen?" in 20:29.

28. Similarly, see Carson, *John*, 418.

29. Cf. the cry (κραυγάζω) of the great Palm Sunday crowd in 12:13. Contrast the cry of his opponents in 18:40; 19:6, 12, 15.

30. He will do so again at the end of the Gospel's second half (11:1–20:31) when in 20:16 he calls Mary by name. See further the name "Mary" only at the beginning of the Gospel's second half in 11:1, 2, 19, 20, 28, 31, 32, 45; 12:3; and at the end of the Gospel's second half in 19:25; 20:1, 11, 16, 18.

31. Cf. the Gospel's only other use of θνῄσκω in 19:33, in both places in the form of a perfect participle, linking the "dead man" who rises here with the "dead man" who rises in John 20.

32. Cf. Revelation 5:2, 12; 6:10; 7:2, 10; 8:13; 10:3; 14:7, 9, 15, 18; 16:17; 19:17.

33. Contrast the bandages of Jesus who requires no such assistance in 20:6–7. As before (see 4:46–54), "Jesus could have healed Lazarus when he was still sick with a word of command, even across the miles. But now he utters a mightier word across a much greater distance—that between the living and the dead." See Rodney A. Whitacre, *John*, IVPNTC 4 (Downers Grove, IL: InterVarsity, 1999), 293. Thus, "Like Lazarus, whose bodily resuscitation becomes John's paradigmatic case, those who hear (οἱ ἀκούσαντες) will live (ζήσουσιν) (Jn 5.25; cf. 11.43-44)," states Deborah Forger, "Jesus as God's Word(s): Aurality, Epistemology, and Embodiment in the Gospel of John," *JSNT* 42 (2020): 286.

that especially the last of Jesus's signs will trigger mass belief in Jesus. They fear a reaction from Rome that will lead to the loss of everything they hold dear (11:47–48). Intending to give counsel, Caiaphas unwittingly prophesies that it is expedient for Jesus to die so that his death might save them all (11:50–52).[34] Therefore, they make plans to put Jesus to death (11:53). They determine that Lazarus too must die (12:9–10).[35] Aware of all of these things, Jesus retreats to Ephraim. There Jesus remains with his disciples (11:54). The Gospel's third and final Passover is at hand. So many go up to Jerusalem beforehand to get ready for the feast (11:55). There in the temple they look for Jesus. There they wait and wonder. Will Jesus come for the feast (11:56) now that an edict has been issued requiring any who know of his whereabouts to assist in his arrest (11:57)? Will the Lamb of God who takes away the sin of the world come?

---

34. The irony would have been "all too apparent to John's readers (especially after A.D. 70): what the Jewish leadership strenuously sought to avoid, namely, for history to repeat itself and for God's judgment to fall on Israel's nation as typified by the temple, is precisely what ensued in the wake of Jesus' crucifixion" (Köstenberger, *John*, 350).

35. So when Jesus dies, he dies because he gave life to Lazarus. He gives life because he dies. See Köstenberger, *John*, 321.

CHAPTER SIX

THE BEGINNING *of* the FINAL WEEK *and the* ARRIVAL *of* HIS HOUR

John 12:1–50

In the story of Jesus that follows (12:1–50), the time for Jesus's fourth and final trip to Jerusalem comes. It is the first day of a six-day-long week that will be the week of the Gospel's third and final Passover.[1] The time for the Lamb of God to take away the sin of the world is nigh. So the Lamb of God comes. But the disciples fail again to comprehend the words and deeds of Jesus. Only later, when Jesus is glorified and on the third day rises, will they remember. Only then will they see. While some enthusiastically receive him at the beginning of the week, others do not. Others refuse the Messenger's message, which is God's word. It affords no light, it gives no sight, to the one who refuses to hear. At the end of the day, Jesus offers one last appeal to those who are with him. And he pledges that the one who continues to believe will most certainly see. Thus, the day ends with its focus on the sole informing sufficiency of the word of the Word Made Flesh to those who would see Jesus as he must be seen. The beginning of the week comes to an end in anticipation of the end of

---

1. Cf. the initial six-day-long week of days in 1:19–2:11, followed by the first of the Gospel's three Passovers in 2:13–25 (see its second and third Passovers in 6:4 and in 11:55; 12:1; 13:1; 18:28, 39; 19:14); and the six-day creation in Genesis 1–2. See further discussion to come on the fundamental importance of the week as basis and framework for the renewal of creation and the promised rest of God.

the week. For only at the end of the week when what Jesus says informs
who Jesus is and what Jesus does will his followers finally see.

"Six days before the Passover" (πρὸ ἓξ ἡμερῶν τοῦ πάσχα, 12:1), six days
before his passion,[2] Jesus comes. Sometime between sundown Friday
night and sundown Saturday night on the Sabbath day that marked the end
of a previous week,[3] Jesus and his disciples arrive in Bethany at the home
of Lazarus and his sisters (see 11:1, 18).[4] There that Saturday night in the
first evening hours of the first day of the week (cf. 20:1, 19, 26) those who
have had their household restored to them welcome Jesus. Together they
share an evening meal (δεῖπνον, 12:2).[5] Martha serves. Lazarus reclines
with Jesus (12:2). And Mary does an extraordinary thing (12:3). There at
table Mary anoints the feet of Jesus with an extravagant quantity[6] of an
exceptionally expensive (πολύτιμος)[7] fragrant ointment (μύρον) made of
pure (πιστικός)[8] nard (νάρδος). Overcome with emotion, full of gratitude

---

2. In both the Synoptics and in John, Jesus is betrayed, arrested, tried, and crucified on the day
of the Passover. He suffers and he dies on the fifteenth of Nisan. See further on the analysis of 13:1;
18:28; and 19:14.

3. "The refrain 'there was evening and there was morning' each day of creation (see Gen 1:5, 8,
13, 19, 23, 31) undergirded the Jewish and Samaritan method of reckoning time, where (each) new
day began with the onset of darkness." See Craig R. Koester, *Symbolism in the Fourth Gospel: Meaning,
Mystery, Community*, 2nd ed. (Minneapolis: Fortress, 2003), 144–45.

4. Both D. A. Carson and Andreas Köstenberger argue that Jesus and his disciples arrived in
Bethany just after sundown Friday night. Carson, *The Gospel according to John*, PNTC (Grand Rapids:
Eerdmans, 1991), 427; Köstenberger, *John*, BECNT (Grand Rapids: Baker Academic, 2004), 359.
J. H. Bernard expresses openness to this possibility, but suggests that they also "may have come only
from a short distance" and therefore could have arrived much later Saturday without "exceeding the
limit of a Sabbath day's journey" (*A Critical and Exegetical Commentary on the Gospel of John*, ICC
[Edinburgh: T&T Clark, 1928], 2:415).

5. No explicit subject for "they made" (ἐποίησαν) in 12:2 is given. "It is possible that someone
else prepared the supper and that Lazarus, Martha, and Mary attended. This is hardly likely, however, given the context and the fact that Martha serves at table," notes Francis J. Moloney, *John*, SP 4
(Collegeville, MN: Liturgical Press, 1998), 356. While a "supper"/"dinner" (δεῖπνον) was the "main
meal of the day," and could begin "as early as the middle of the afternoon," here the meal follows the
Sabbath and so was an evening meal that was quite possibly "connected with the *Habdalah* service,
which marked the end of the Sabbath" (Köstenberger, *John*, 360).

6. See "pound" in 12:3. A (Roman) pound (λίτρα), observes Köstenberger, *John*, 360, "amounted
to about eleven ounces." See the noun elsewhere in the Greek of the LXX and New Testament only
in 19:39. Both then and today, what she uses to anoint him is "a very large amount.".

7. See elsewhere in the Greek of the LXX and New Testament "precious"/"expensive"/"costly"
(πολύτιμος) only in Jesus's parable of the pearl of great price (Matt 13:46) and in 1 Peter 1:7.

8. See elsewhere in the Greek of the LXX and New Testament "pure" (πιστικός) only in Mark
14:3, where it also describes an expensive ointment of pure nard, but the ointment is applied to
Jesus's head.

and joy, thinking only of her need to show Jesus the breadth and depth of her love and devotion, Mary anoints Jesus's feet and wipes[9] them with her hair (cf. 11:2).[10]

All societal definitions of propriety are seemingly suspended.[11] What normally restrains or inhibits does not. Mary does not care what the others may think. Nothing she does is unseemly or immodest. Nothing is beneath her. No gift is too great. She holds back nothing. Love irrepressible owns her. Like no other love, it governs her every impulse. Love amazing, love divine, demands her soul, her life, her all. As radical as it all may seem and is, Mary believes that she has every reason to respond to Jesus as she does. Never before has she had such overwhelming feelings. At no time has she ever wanted to belong to a person the way that she wants to belong to Jesus. Never has there been such a man. How right she is to believe that belonging to him is everything. How right she is to want the perfume that perfumes him to perfume her.[12] How right will all things be when the end comes and what defines him defines her in the house that God's end-time Bridegroom[13] has come to claim as his own.[14] All will be as it should be when, in the end, the

---

9. See elsewhere "wipe" (ἐκμάσσω) only in 11:2 and in 13:5.

10. "Anointing the head was common enough (Ps 23:5; Luke 7:46), but anointing the feet was quite unusual" (Köstenberger, *John*, 361). Wiping his feet with her hair was even more unusual. "After an anointing, the oil is not normally wiped off" (Herman Ridderbos, *The Gospel of John: A Theological Commentary*, trans. John Vriend [Grand Rapids: Eerdmans, 1997], 415n111). And Jewish women "never unbound their hair in public," adds Köstenberger, *John*, 362. "The fact that Mary (who probably was single, as no husband is mentioned) here acts in such a way toward Jesus, a well-known (yet unattached) rabbi, was sure to raise some eyebrows." For the suggestion that her actions could easily have been seen as a provocative advance, see Craig Blomberg, *The Historical Reliability of John's Gospel: Issues and Commentary* (Downers Grove, IL: InterVarsity, 2001), 177.

11. "Devotion takes precedence over convention." Cornelis Bennema, *Encountering Jesus: Character Studies in the Gospel of John*, 2nd ed. (Minneapolis: Fortress, 2014), 271.

12. What she uses to anoint his feet she transfers to her own head when she wipes his feet with her hair. Cf. the comment of Theodore of Mopsuestia, cited by J. F. Coakley, "The Anointing at Bethany and the Priority of John," *JBL* 107 (1988): 252: "For it was as if the woman planned this so as to attach the fragrance of our Lord's flesh to her body. For she took care that she should always be with him: she did this in her love so that if she should come to be separated from him, by this she could suppose that he was with her still."

13. That Mary "anoints" (ἀλείφω) Jesus is consistent also with his identity as Messiah and King. See ἀλείφω elsewhere in the Gospel only in 11:2.

14. For the suggestion that first-century romantic settings were often associated with a woman's anointing of a man's feet with perfume and that Jesus's identity as Bridegroom, her wiping of his feet with her hair, and his love for Mary, Martha, and Lazarus (11:5) all indicate that Mary of Bethany is portrayed here as the bride of Jesus, see Adeline Fehribach, *The Women in the Life of the Bridegroom:*

fragrance (ὀσμή) of Jesus fills (πληρόω)[15] the entire house (οἰκία) where
he and they are (12:3). As before "in the beginning" (1:1), all things will
be "very good" (LXX Gen 1:31) once more when the fragrance of Jesus
extends to—when it permeates and defines—everyone and everything.[16]
At the end of the week, Jesus will give them all even greater reasons to
be fanatically devoted to him. At yet another evening meal (δεῖπνον, 13:2,
4; 21:20),[17] Jesus will show his followers what true love is when he turns
his attention to their feet (13:2–11). His humble act, his self-sacrificing
example (13:12–15; see also 13:35; 15:9–13), will foreshadow the unrivaled
extravagance of what he does next. When the time comes, the Lamb of
God who takes away the sin of the world will offer the sacrifice to end
all sacrifice. His will be the Passover to end all Passovers.

Mary's extravagance offends. Judas objects. But Judas has self-motivated
reasons for doing so. Judas covets what he would have possessed as the
keeper of their shared funds had the ointment been sold for as much as
three hundred denarii[18] (12:3–6). Judas was a thief.[19] But Jesus welcomes
Mary's extraordinary gesture. For her actions bespeak again a truth that
is greater than she or they are ready to see. At the end of the week, the
exquisite fragrance (ὀσμή) of the Lamb of God's sacrifice of himself will
come. His sacrifice will make all things full.[20] And Mary will belong to
Jesus. They all will belong to him. They all will be his Bride (3:29), in

---

A Feminist Historical-Literary Analysis of the Female Characters in the Fourth Gospel (Collegeville, MN: Liturgical Press, 1998), 89.

15. The verb appears twice in John 1–11 (see 3:29; 7:8) and thirteen times in John 12–19.

16. Cf. Christ's giving up of himself as "a fragrant offering and sacrifice to God" in Ephesians 5:2. See also the only other use of ὀσμή in the New Testament in Philemon 4:18; 2 Corinthians 2:14, 16. Contrast Lazarus and the stench of decay in 11:39. "Fragrance" (ὀσμή) is especially frequent in Leviticus and Numbers where tabernacle, priests, and sacrifice are a dominant interest. See further the sacrifice of Noah in LXX Genesis 8:21; and the fragrance of the garments of Jacob in LXX Genesis 27:27.

17. Cf. the δεῖπνον of the marriage feast of the Lamb in Revelation 19:9, 17.

18. "Three hundred denarii" corresponds roughly to a year's wages for an average day laborer. "The perfume was outrageously expensive," an especially rare and precious commodity that was "imported all the way from northern India. Its great value may indicate that Mary and her family were very wealthy" (Köstenberger, John, 363).

19. It is John alone who mentions that Judas was a κλέπτης ("thief," 12:6). Cf. the Gospel's only other use of the noun in 10:1, 8, 10.

20. See elsewhere the making full of all things by Jesus especially in 19:28–30.

his house (8:35; 14:2–3).[21] So Jesus points to the greater significance of her actions. He interprets what she has done as preparation for burial (ἐνταφιασμός, 12:7).

Mary does these things on the tenth of Nisan.[22] She does them when, according to Exodus 12:2–5, each Jewish household would have selected and kept with it a lamb to be given in sacrifice and consumed at table five days later in the evening hours of the fifteenth of Nisan (see Exod 12:6–14). Each year, then, a lamb was eaten in the evening hours of a sixth day that was rich with ritual and was called the Passover. Therefore, Mary unwittingly does these things on the tenth of Nisan because the time has come for each Jewish household to select and keep with it a lamb. She does these things because at the end of the week the time will come for the Lamb of God to offer himself up in paschal sacrifice for the sin of the world.[23] When that day comes the lifeless body of Jesus will be readied again for burial[24] and laid into a tomb (19:38–42).[25] But at the beginning of the week none of Jesus's followers see any of this in any of Mary's actions. None of them see any aspect of it in her actions or in Jesus's words (12:7). Not one of them sees Jesus as he must be seen.

---

21. Thus, the language of both 12:1–7 and 19:38–42 (see further below) is especially reminiscent also of the language of the Song of Songs and its central figure who, like Jesus, is bridegroom, shepherd, and king. See the references to an "ointment" (μύρον), "nard" (νάρδος, elsewhere in the Greek of the LXX and New Testament only in Mark 14:3), and "fragrance" (ὀσμή) in LXX Song of Songs 1:3–4, 12; 2:13; 4:10–14; 7:9, 14. See also "bridegroom" and "bride" and the "fragrance of ointment" in LXX Jeremiah 25:10.

22. Jesus and his disciples arrive in Bethany "six days before the Passover" (12:1). The fifteenth of Nisan is the day of the Passover. Six days before the fifteenth of Nisan is the 9th of Nisan. The dinner that they share that night takes place in the first evening hours of the tenth of Nisan. See Armand J. Gagne Jr., "An Examination and Possible Explanation of John's Dating of the Crucifixion," in *The Death of Jesus in the Fourth Gospel*, ed. Gilbert Van Belle, BETL 200 (Leuven: Leuven University Press, 2007), 417. See further on the Gospel's chronology of the passion in the analysis of 13:1; 18:28; and 19:14.

23. Jesus's sacrifice will be a paschal sacrifice. It will also be *more* than a paschal sacrifice. See above the analysis of 1:29. See further William C. Weinrich, *John 1:1–7:1*, ConcC (St. Louis: Concordia, 2015), 237–49; and Richard Bauckham, *Gospel of Glory: Major Themes in Johannine Theology* (Grand Rapids: Baker Academic, 2015), 154–59.

24. Cf. "prepare for burial" (ἐνταφιάζω) in 19:40. See further the use of an "ointment" (μύρον) to prepare the body of Jesus for burial in Luke 23:56; to anoint the tent of meeting and the ark of the testimony in LXX Exodus 30:25–26; to anoint Aaron in LXX Psalm 132:2; and those for whom the Lord of Hosts makes a mountaintop feast for all the nations in LXX Isaiah 25:6–7.

25. See further Bruce G. Schuchard, "Form versus Function: Citation Technique and Authorial Intention in the Gospel of John," in *Abiding Words: The Use of Scripture in the Gospel of John*, ed. Alicia D. Myers and Bruce G. Schuchard, RBS 81 (Atlanta: SBL Press, 2015), 37–38.

When the crowds hear that Jesus is in the vicinity of Jerusalem, they come not only to see Jesus but also to see Lazarus (12:9). So the chief priests also make plans to put Lazarus to death (12:10–11). The next day,[26] the large crowd that has come to Jerusalem for the sake of the feast hears that Jesus is coming (12:12). So they take palm branches and go out to meet him, saying, "Hosanna! Blessed is he who comes in the name of the Lord, even the King of Israel!" (12:13). Responding, Jesus finds and mounts a donkey. For it is written, "Fear not, daughter Zion; behold, your king is coming, sitting on the foal of a donkey [ἐπὶ πῶλον ὄνου]" (12:14–15).[27] His disciples fail again to comprehend any of this while it is happening. But a day of clarity will come. It will come soon. When on the cross Jesus is glorified and on the third day he rises (2:19), then will they remember (12:16; cf. 2:22; 8:28). Then will they see. Word of the raising of Lazarus continues to spread (12:17–18).[28] And the Pharisees ironically see that, unless they make good on their plans to put Jesus to death, all the world will go after him (12:19).

Greeks who also have come to Jerusalem for the sake of the feast come next. They ask to see Jesus (12:20–21).[29] Jesus marks the significance of their coming together with everything else that has recently happened. He marks the following: a troubled Thomas and a dead man who rises (cf. 20:1–29); the beginning of a six-day-long paschal week that will end with

---

26. Here, the words τῇ ἐπαύριον, frequently translated "on the next day," refer not to a next calendar day (as in 1:29, 35, 43) but to the daylight hours that followed on the same calendar day. Similarly, see 6:22. Therefore, "the next day" is Sunday morning. "The next day" is still the first day of the week (cf. 20:1, 19).

27. Cf. the blessing given by Jacob to his son Judah in LXX Genesis 49:10–11: "A ruler shall not fail from Judah, nor one who reigns from his loins, until the things stored up for him come, and he is the expectation of the nations. Binding his foal to the vine, and the foal of his donkey [τὸν πῶλον τῆς ὄνου αὐτοῦ] to the branch, he shall wash his robe in wine, and his garment in the blood of the grape." The phrase "foal of a donkey" appears nowhere else in the Greek of the LXX and New Testament. See further Jesus's manner of invoking Zechariah 9:9–10 and its meek king who mounts a donkey and speaks not of war but of peace as an affirming yet informing reaction to the nationalism of the people inherent in their use of palms and in their words from Psalm 118 (LXX 117) in Bruce G. Schuchard, *Scripture within Scripture: The Interrelationship of Form and Function in the Explicit Old Testament Citations in the Gospel of John*, SBLDS 133 (Atlanta: Scholars Press, 1992), 71–84.

28. Köstenberger, *John*, 357n3, observes nicely that Lazarus is thus mentioned in John 12 at the beginning of the chapter (12:1–2), at the conclusion of its account of the anointing (12:9–11), and at the conclusion of the triumphal entry (12:17–19).

29. See "Greeks" ("Ελλην) elsewhere only in 7:35. "As elsewhere in the NT," the designation "refers not necessarily to people literally hailing from Greece but to Gentiles from any part of the Greek-speaking world." Köstenberger, *John*, 377.

the paschal giving of the Lamb of God who takes away the sin of the world (cf. 13:1; 18:28; 19:14); an evening meal (cf. 13:2); the anointing of Jesus's feet (cf. 13:4–17; see also 1:27) as preparation for burial (cf. 19:38–42); the reaction of Judas, the keeper of the common funds (cf. 13:2, 21–30); Jesus's final trip to Jerusalem, the crowd's reception of him there, and his reaction to them; the fear of the opposition and their determination to put him to death; and, last, the coming of the Greeks (see Isa 49:6). All of these things encourage Jesus fittingly to announce that the fateful hour (ὥρα) for the Son of Man to be glorified has finally come (12:23; cf. 7:39; 12:16).[30]

Jesus speaks further of his impending death. And he invites those who would serve him to follow (12:24–26). As before, Jesus is troubled (cf. 11:33; 13:21). But he also expresses his resolve. For the purpose of his hour he has come (12:27), an hour that will span a week (see 17:1). In their hearing, he therefore prays to his Father. Jesus asks that with the accomplishment of his hour the Father's name (ὄνομα) would be glorified. A voice from heaven responds, saying, "I have glorified [ἐδόξασα] [it] and I will glorify [δοξάσω] [it] again" (12:28). Those present hear this. But, again, they fail to comprehend it. Some think that what they have heard is thunder. Others suggest that a heavenly messenger has spoken (12:29). Again, Jesus attempts to explain. He suggests that the voice has spoken not for his sake but for their sake (12:30). For the time for judgment (κρίσις) has come. The time has come for the ruler (ἄρχων) of this world (cf. 14:30; 16:11) to be cast out (ἐκβάλλω) (12:31).

"When I am lifted up [ὑψόω; cf. 3:14; 8:28; 12:34] from the earth [on the cross]," declares Jesus, "I will draw [ἕλκω] all [of the persons of this world] to myself" (12:32). He says this to signify (σημαίνω)[31] the manner of his dying (12:33).[32] But, once again, they fail to comprehend him. Some object. According to their understanding of God's word, the Christ remains forever. So they ask, "How can you say that the Son of Man must be lifted up? Who is this Son of Man?" (12:34). The word of the Word Made Flesh

---

30. See further Köstenberger, *John*, 378.

31. See the consistent force of σημαίνω (signify) in 18:32; 21:19. Cf. the consistently foreshadowing nature of Jesus's signs (σημεῖον).

32. Thus, the moment of his glorification, his exaltation, his lifting up, and his return to the Father are all the same moment, the moment of his suffering and death on the cross.

is for them an inexplicable conundrum.[33] Even so, Jesus urges them to walk in the light of his word for the little while (μικρὸς χρόνος) that it— that he—is still with them (12:35).[34] "While you have the Light," declares Jesus, "believe in the Light, that you may be sons of light" (12:36). When Jesus finishes saying these things, he leaves. In keeping with what will soon transpire, he hides himself from them.

They have seen much. They have heard much. Yet many refuse to believe (12:37). They do so in fulfillment[35] of the prophecy of Isaiah, who said, "Lord, who has believed our *report*?" (12:38).[36] Who has believed the Messenger's message, which is God's word? It affords no light—it gives no sight—to the one who refuses to hear (cf. 3:19–21).[37] Instead, paradoxically, the Messenger's message (12:38), which is the word of the Word Made Flesh, "has blinded their eyes," says the Lord (through Isaiah).[38] "It has hardened their heart, lest they see with their eyes, and comprehend with their heart, and turn (cf. 20:16), and I heal them" (12:40).

---

33. Leon Morris observes, "To the end, they remain confused and perplexed, totally unable to appreciate the magnitude of the gift offered to them and the significance of the Person who offers it." *The Gospel according to John*, rev. ed., NICNT (Grand Rapids: Eerdmans, 1995), 533.

34. See also a "little while" in 7:33; 13:33; 14:19; 16:16–19.

35. For John's first use here of πληρόω (fulfill) to indicate the fulfillment of Old Testament prophecy, see Schuchard, *Scripture within Scripture*, 86–87 (citing others). Beginning with John 12:38 each subsequent citation of the Old Testament in the Gospel includes a similar explicit reference to the fulfillment of Scripture. See 13:18; 15:25; 19:24, 36–37.

36. Cf. the complaint of Moses, who begs Israel to hear in LXX Deuteronomy 29:1–30:20. See further the Gospel's citation of LXX Isaiah 53:1 in Schuchard, *Scripture within Scripture*, 85–90.

37. "No one sees or responds to Jesus unless they are taught or drawn by God, unless their eyes are [thus] opened to see," explains Marianne Meye Thompson, *John: A Commentary*, NTL (Louisville: Westminster John Knox, 2015), 274. See 6:44–45, 60–69.

38. The citation's initial verb, τετύφλωκεν, is third-person singular. From context one must infer an appropriate subject. In John's Gospel, what blinds is not God, or Jesus, or even the devil. What blinds is the light (3:19–21; cf. the darkness in 1 John 2:11). What blinds is the Messenger's report (12:38). What blinds, then, is the word of the Word Made Flesh. Just as the prophetic word of Isaiah was rejected, observes Ridderbos, *John*, 444, so was the word of the Word Made Flesh. See also Ardel Caneday, "The Word Made Flesh as Mystery Incarnate: Revealing and Concealing Dramatized by Jesus as Portrayed in John's Gospel," *JETS* 60 (2017): 762–64. Cf. Craig R. Koester, *Symbolism in the Fourth Gospel: Meaning, Mystery, Community*, 2nd ed. (Minneapolis: Fortress, 2003), 70. For Koester, "the light of truth is like the light of the sun. Its radiance enables some to see, yet it can blind those who stare into it without blinking." See elsewhere according to Isaiah the necessity of hearing and the blindness that results when one refuses to do so (especially "they have closed their eyes" in LXX Isa 6:10) in Matthew 13:13–16 and Acts 28:23–28. See further the Gospel's citation here of Isaiah in Schuchard, *Scripture within Scripture*, 91–106.

Later, at the close of the day, Jesus offers one last appeal to those who are with him. And he pledges that the one who continues to believe will most certainly see. (12:44–45). The Light of the World comes so that all who believe may no longer dwell in darkness (12:46). He who hears the word of the Word Made Flesh and rejects that word has a judge. His judge will be the very Word that he has rejected (12:47–48). Jesus speaks not on his own but says what the Father who sent him has instructed him to say (12:49).[39] Therefore, his instruction (ἐντολή),[40] his word, is everything. Upon it all things hinge. With its concluding focus, then, on the sole informing sufficiency of the word of the Word Made Flesh to those who would see Jesus as he must be seen, the Gospel's narrative of the beginning of its final week comes to an end. It comes to an end in anticipation of the end of the week. For only at the end of the week when what Jesus says informs who Jesus is and what Jesus does will clarity come. Only when the word of the Word Made Flesh informs both his person and his purpose will it then be possible to see Jesus as finally he must be seen.[41]

---

39. Therefore, "how one has responded to Jesus' word determines what judgment will be passed because this word has come from the Father and has been spoken by the embodied Word of God" (Thompson, *John*, 277).

40. See ἐντολή in the singular and in the plural with no great difference in meaning between the two in 10:18; 11:57; 12:49, 50; 13:34; 14:15, 21; 15:10, 12. See also 1 John 2:3–8; 2 John 5. Here and elsewhere, Jesus repeatedly refers not to a "commandment" or "commandments" but more broadly to the instruction of God that is light and sight to the one who believes. See further Bruce G. Schuchard, *1–3 John*, ConcC (Saint Louis: Concordia, 2012), 151–96.

41. For mere "seeing does not guarantee understanding or insight" (Thompson, *John*, 276). In the Gospel, sight only becomes insight through instruction "following the resurrection of Jesus, and under the tutelage of the Holy Spirit."

CHAPTER SEVEN

THE END *of the* FINAL WEEK *and the* ACCOMPLISHMENT *of* HIS HOUR

John 13:1–19:42

I n the story of Jesus that follows, the end of the week and the time for the finality of Jesus's hour comes. At table again, Jesus shows his disciples the full extent of his love. He foreshadows what is next and what it will mean. And he readies them for it. "If I go [to the cross]," declares Jesus, "and [there] prepare a place for you, I will come again" (14:3). He will rise and return to them. "I will ask the Father," adds Jesus, "and he will give you another Paraclete" (14:16). He will give "the Spirit of Truth" (14:17). For the God that no one has ever seen can only be seen by the one who sees Jesus as he must be seen. But the seeing of Jesus as he must be seen can only be done by the one who hears what must be heard. Therefore, "when the Paraclete comes," declares Jesus, "he will teach you all things and bring to your remembrance everything that I have said to you" (14:26). Then and only then will they see. "He will *guide you into all truth*," adds Jesus (16:13). For he is the Spirit of Truth. "Everyone who is of the truth hears my voice," declares Jesus (18:37). Only the one who hears Jesus sees Jesus. Only the one who sees Jesus sees God.

"Before the Feast of the Passover" (πρὸ τῆς ἑορτῆς τοῦ πάσχα, 13:1), at the beginning of Jesus's fated final week (12:2–50), Jesus knew already "that his hour [ὥρα] had come to depart this world to return to the Father"

(13:1a). So at the beginning of the week Jesus announces that his hour has come (12:23),[1] knowing what his hour will require of him when the end comes. At the end of the week, because Jesus loves "his own" (τοὺς ἰδίους)[2] who are in the world, he will love them "to the end" (εἰς τέλος) (13:1b).[3] In every way he will display the full extent of his love. To the utmost, he will love. To the completion of the end that is his purpose for descending to this world from heaven above, he will do what he must do. For the sake of the endpoint of the messianic task that is his alone to achieve, he will stay the course. So the law of Moses might fittingly see its end and thus come to an end,[4] he will see his mission to its end.[5] In every way he will display what it means to love.

What follows moves, then, in rather spectacular fashion from a first day at the beginning of the week (12:2–50) to a sixth and final day at the end of the week (13:2–19:42). *Nothing* is said of days two through five. Instead, the focus is entirely on days one and six so each might inform the other. The end informs the beginning. The beginning informs the end.[6] Therefore, once more (cf. 12:2), the end begins with a meal (13:2). In the early evening hours of the fifteenth of Nisan,[7] at its Passover meal (see δείπνου γινομένου in 13:2),[8] Jesus rises and lays down (τίθημι)[9]

---

1. See "the hour has come" in 12:23. See also Jesus's foreknowledge of his imminent departure in 12:27, 31–36. Thus, the initial time-marking prepositional phrase "before the feast of the Passover" (πρὸ τῆς ἑορτῆς τοῦ πάσχα) in 13:1a modifies not the verb of the sentence's concluding clause ("he loved them to the end") but the participle εἰδώς ("knowing") that follows immediately after πρὸ τῆς ἑορτῆς τοῦ πάσχα.

2. Cf. "he came to his own" (1:11); and "he calls his own" (10:3–4).

3. Thus, 13:1 links, bridges, and marks both the beginning and the end of Jesus' fated final week. And it informs the fundamental relationship of John 12 (the tenth of Nisan) to John 13–19 (the fifteenth of Nisan).

4. See above the analysis of 1:17.

5. Therefore, when from the cross Jesus declares, "It is finished" (19:30), he proclaims regarding the full extent of his love that its *"telos* has been reached." See Craig R. Koester, *The Word of Life: A Theology of John's Gospel* (Grand Rapids: Eerdmans, 2008), 111.

6. In fact, fully a third of the narrative of the Gospel (John 13–19) is devoted to its extended description of the fated, final twenty-four-hour period of time that was the day when the paschal hour of the Lamb of God who takes away the sin of the world (1:29) saw its end.

7. See above the analysis of "six days before the Passover" in 12:1.

8. The genitive absolute δείπνου γινομένου in 13:2 bears a time sense equivalent to that of its sentence's main verb, the historical present ἐγείρεται ("he rose [up from the dinner]"), in 13:4, and is best understood as the equivalent of a temporal clause ("while dinner was happening").

9. Cf. (also with τίθημι) the laying down of the life of the Good Shepherd in 10:11, 15, 17, 18. Later, the order of his rising and laying down is reversed. First he lays down his life. Then he rises.

his (outer) garments (13:3–4).[10] Girding himself with a servant's towel (λέντιον),[11] he pours water into a washbasin (νιπτήρ),[12] washes the feet of his disciples, and wipes[13] their feet with the towel (13:4–5). In now characteristic fashion, Peter unwittingly objects (13:6). Jesus responds, assuring Peter that what he is not seeing now he will see later (13:7).[14] But Peter persists. And so Jesus says, "If I do not wash you, you have no part in me" (13:8). Persisting still, Peter attempts to alter the nature of the bath that Jesus is telling him he must receive (13:9).[15] Jesus refuses Peter's enduringly unwitting interest and instead insists on the necessity of what he must do (13:10). To be with Jesus is to be entirely (ὅλος) clean (καθαρός).[16] Jesus washes their feet not because his disciples are not yet clean. He washes their feet so that later they may finally see the necessity of cruciform love.

Not all, however, are clean (13:10). For Jesus knows who his betrayer will be (13:11). Therefore, when finished with washing their feet, Jesus takes up[17] his garments and resumes his place. And Jesus asks, "Do you know what I have done for you? You call me Teacher [διδάσκαλος] and Lord [κύριος]. And you speak well. For I am [εἰμί] [both of these things]" (13:12–13). "I have given you an example [ὑπόδειγμα]," adds Jesus (13:15). He has shown them what soon he will do. He will lay down his life for

---

10. See further the garments (ἱμάτια) of Jesus in 19:5, 24–25.

11. "Towel" (λέντιον) appears only here in the Greek of the LXX and New Testament.

12. "Washbasin" (νιπτήρ) appears only here in the Greek of the LXX and New Testament.

13. Cf. "wipe" (ἐκμάσσω) here and in 11:2; 12:3.

14. What Peter fails for now to see, is that "the basis of the cleansing foreshadowed by the washing of his feet lay ahead in the hideous ignominy of the barbarous cross" (D. A. Carson, *The Gospel according to John*, PNTC [Grand Rapids: Eerdmans, 1991], 464). Thus, "what Jesus says to Peter about purification makes the footwashing a symbol for Jesus' act of total purification in his surrender for his own on the cross" (Herman Ridderbos, *The Gospel of John: A Theological Commentary*, trans. John Vriend [Grand Rapids: Eerdmans, 1997], 464).

15. Specifically, Peter says, "Lord, not my feet only but also my hands and my head."

16. When Jesus responds to Peter's words "Lord, not my feet only but also my hands and my head" in 13:9 and says in 13:10, "the one who has bathed does not need to wash … but is entirely clean," he likely recalls the custom "for guests at a meal to take a bath before leaving home, and on arrival at their host's house to have their feet, but only their feet, washed" (Charles K. Barrett, *The Gospel according to St. John*, 2nd ed. [Philadelphia: Westminster, 1978], 441). Thus, Jesus suggests to his disciples that he washes their feet not because they are not yet clean but for another reason.

17. Cf. (also with λαμβάνω) the taking up again of the life of the Good Shepherd in 10:17–18. Thus, "John links the footwashing with Jesus' sacrificial death" (Andreas Köstenberger, *John*, BECNT [Grand Rapids: Baker Academic, 2004], 404).

the life of the world (cf. 10:11, 14–15, 17–18).[18] Not only will he do this. They too will do this. For "a servant [δοῦλος] is not greater than his lord. Neither is a sent one [ἀπόστολος][19] greater than the one who sent him" (13:16). Therefore, they too will be as is he. They too will be sent ones (4:38; 17:18; 20:21), apostles (13:16), in the stead and by the command of their Sender. "If you know these things," concludes Jesus—if they see in these things what must be seen—"blessed [μακάριοι] are you if you do them" (13:17).[20] Blessed are they if what defines him defines them. Blessed are they if theirs is the love of the one who loved us first (1 John 4:19).[21]

Jesus does not speak of all of them. He knows who his betrayer is (13:18). Jesus says these things before they happen—before the disciples are ready to see—so when they happen the disciples will remember. Then will the disciples see (cf. 2:22; 8:28; 12:16). "I say it now," pledges Jesus, "so that later you may believe [and see] that I am [he] [ἐγώ εἰμι]" (13:19). He says it now so that later others will also hear and believe when they hear from the Sent One's sent ones. Others too will hear and receive both the Sent One and the Sender of the Sent One (13:20).

When Jesus finishes saying these things, he is deeply—he is profoundly—troubled (cf. 11:33; 12:27). Once more, he who knows all things (2:24–25) knows what soon will be. And so Jesus says, "One of you will betray me!" (13:21). Uncertain and confused,[22] the disciples wonder who this could be (13:22). The Beloved Disciple[23] is reclining in the bosom

---

18. See Koester, *Word of Life*, 111.

19. "Sent one" (ἀπόστολος) appears only here in the Gospel. See, however, Revelation 2:2; 18:20; 21:14.

20. Cf. "blessed are those who have not seen and yet have believed" what must in the end be seen in 20:29. The only other macarism in the Gospel is in 13:17.

21. See their need to "love one another as I have loved you" in 15:12. Thus, Jesus's "act of humility is as unnecessary as it is stunning, and is simultaneously a display of love (v. 1), a symbol of saving cleansing (vv. 6–9), and a model of Christian conduct (vv. 12–17)" (Carson, *John*, 462–63).

22. The verb ἀπορέω ("be at a loss," "be perplexed") appears nowhere else in this Gospel. Cf. its use in Mark 6:20; Luke 24:4; Acts 25:20; 2 Cor 4:8; Gal 4:20.

23. For the first time, the Evangelist, who has refrained thus far from explicitly identifying himself in the telling of his story (see the anonymous one in 1:35–40), describes himself here not as a person with a name but as the disciple whom Jesus loved. See further the anonymity of the Evangelist in 18:15–16 (where we hear only of "another disciple"; see also 20:2, 3, 4, 8); 19:26–27 (see also v. 35); 20:2–10; 21:1–14 (where in v. 2 we hear only of the nameless "[sons] of Zebedee" [οἱ τοῦ Ζεβεδαίου]; cf. the "disciple whom Jesus loved" in v. 7); and 21:20–24 (where he is still not named but is identified as the Gospel's author). He does this not to conceal his identity. "Doubtless his recipients knew him well," observes Köstenberger, *John*, 414.

(κόλπος) of Jesus (13:23; cf. 1:18).²⁴ So Peter encourages the Beloved Disciple to inquire after the identity of the betrayer (13:24). Jesus says that by means of a gesture with a morsel of bread (ψωμίον)²⁵ he will show them who his betrayer is. As he has before, Jesus tells them how to understand his gesture when they see it (13:26). But they do not understand. So when Jesus says to Judas, "What you are about to do, do quickly" (13:27), no one knows or sees why (13:28). The unwitting possibilities that they consider are once more far from the mark of what Jesus would have them see (13:29). Judas departs. And it is night (νύξ) (13:30).²⁶

The hour when Jesus will be glorified is nigh (13:31–32). So Jesus speaks again of his hour. "Children [τεκνία],"²⁷ declares Jesus, "only a little while [longer] will I be with you.²⁸ You will seek me. But ... where I am going you cannot come" (13:33).²⁹ They will seek him. But only he will go to the cross. Only he will rest in the grave. He alone will rise (2:19). When he does so, a new (καινός) kind of instruction (ἐντολή),³⁰ a new Torah of the Word Made Flesh (cf. 1:17; see further Gal 6:2; Rom 8:2) will come. When it comes, his life-giving example, his self-giving love, will inform theirs. So Jesus instructs his disciples to "love one another just as I have loved you" (13:34).³¹ In this way, the world will know that they are his disciples, when

---

24. Cf. the bosom (κόλπος) of the Father in 1:18; and the bosom of Abraham in Luke 16:22–23. "Hence, the present passage legitimizes and authorizes the author of the present Gospel and the testimony contained therein," observes Köstenberger, *John*, 414. See also Ridderbos, *John*, 470.

25. The vocable ψωμίον (morsel of bread) appears only here in the Greek of the LXX and New Testament.

26. Köstenberger, *John*, 418, notes the reference to "night" (νύξ) likely "conveys the notion of spiritual darkness entered by the betrayer (cf. Luke 22:53: 'this is your hour—when darkness reigns')." Cf. "night is coming" in 9:4. See also 3:2; 11:10; 19:39; 21:3.

27. The vocable τεκνίον appears only here (cf. 1 John 2:1, 12, 28; 3:18; 4:4; 5:21). See, however, the synonyms τέκνον in 1:12; 8:39; 11:52 (cf. 1 John 3:1, 2, 10; 5:2; 2 John 1:1, 4, 13; 3 John 1:4); and παιδίον in 4:49; 16:21; 21:5 (cf. 1 John 2:14, 18; 3:7).

28. See also "a little while" in 7:33; 12:35; 14:19; 16:16–19.

29. With what follows, "Jesus prepares his followers for the difficult times ahead. The present section resembles the genre of farewell discourse. Patterned after Moses' farewell discourse in Deuteronomy (31–32) and other similar OT farewells, an entire genre of such works emerged during the Second Temple period," Köstenberger, *John*, 396.

30. Again, Jesus refers not to a "commandment" or "commandments" (cf. 12:49–50) but more broadly to the instruction of God that is light and sight to the one who believes. Cf. 1 John 2:3–8; 2 John 5. See further Bruce G. Schuchard, *1–3 John*, ConcC (Saint Louis: Concordia, 2012), 151–96.

31. Therefore, what is "new" is "Jesus' command for his disciples to love one another *as he has loved them*" (Köstenberger, *John*, 423). What is new is what the love of Jesus alone has power to accomplish. Cf. Revelation 2:17; 3:12; 5:9; 14:3; 21:1, 2, 5.

theirs is the love of Jesus (13:35; cf. 1 John 4:19). Peter and the others are perplexed. And so Peter asks, "Lord, where are you going?" Jesus responds, saying, "You cannot follow me now. But you will follow me later" (13:36). Peter responds again with a truth that is greater than he knows, saying, "Lord, why can I not follow you now? I will lay down my life for you" (13:37; cf. 21:18–19). "Will you?" asks Jesus. "Really?" Not at first will he do so. First, declares Jesus, "you will deny me three times" (13:38).

Jesus seeks to comfort. He attempts to inform. "Let not your hearts be troubled,"[32] says Jesus. "Believe in God. Believe also in me.[33] In the house[hold] [ἐν τῇ οἰκίᾳ][34] of my Father are many dwelling places [μοναί; see also 14:23].[35] If it were not so, would I have told you that I go to prepare a place [τόπον] for you?" (14:1–2).[36] He has not explicitly spoken of preparing a place until now. But he has repeatedly spoken of "going," "leaving," "departing." "And if I go," adds Jesus, "and [by my dying] prepare a place for you, I will come again [I will rise and return to you]. I will take you to myself so that where I am you also may be" (14:3).

Jesus has spoken often of his impending death. And so Jesus says, "Where I am going, you know the way [ὁδόν]" (14:4).[37] But they have understood precious little. So Thomas speaks for the second time (cf. 11:16) for the company of his fellow disciples (11:16). And Thomas says, "Lord, we do not know where you are going. How are we able to know the way?" (14:5).[38] Talk of the cross is presently too much for them. So

---

32. "In keeping with Semitic anthropology," heart describes "the seat of a person's will and emotions" (Köstenberger, *John*, 425). The combination of μή plus the present imperative ταρασσέσθω suggests that the disciples are already troubled and that Jesus is encouraging them to stop. See James W. Voelz, *Fundamental Greek Grammar*, 2nd ed. (St. Louis, Concordia, 1993), 219.

33. In the absence of understanding, what remains for the disciples is the necessity of trust until greater understanding informs and affirms trust.

34. Cf. 4:53; 8:35; 2 John 10.

35. The vocable μονή appears only here and in 14:23 in the Greek of the LXX and New Testament. Again, in Jesus what defines him ("temple" [2:19, 21] and "house" [cf. 2:16]) defines them. They are the dwelling place of the Lord (1:14; see also Rev 7:15; 21:3). They are God's house, where only a son (see 1:12–13; 11:52; 13:33; 21:5; see also "go to my brothers" in 20:17) and not a slave dwells in the age that is to come (8:35). See further on the analysis of 19:25–27.

36. Thus, there may be irony "in the fact that the Jews fear that their 'place' will be taken away from them by the Romans (11:48)," a fear that was realized in AD 70, "while Jesus' disciples can look forward to a 'place' prepared for them by their master" (Köstenberger, *John*, 427).

37. Cf. "make straight the way" in 1:23. See further the early followers of the Way in Acts 9:2; 19:9, 23; 22:4; 24:14, 22.

38. See Ridderbos, *John*, 493. See also Köstenberger, *John*, 428.

Jesus speaks of what will be when he traverses the way that is set for him alone. "I am the Way and the Truth and the Life," say Jesus. "No one comes to the Father except through me. If you had known me, you also would have known my Father" (14:6–7a; cf. 1:18). In truth, the day will come, and soon, when they will see what fails them now. And so Jesus says, "Even now you know him and have seen him" (14:7b). They have seen and heard what they must know. When they see better because they finally hear better, then will Jesus's words inform and his form be seen as that of the God that they must see (1:18).

Like Thomas (14:5; see also 11:16), Philip too speaks on behalf of the others. And he ironically says, "Lord, show *us* the Father, and it will suffice for *us*" (14:8).[39] For they know but do not know. They see but do not see. The day will come when finally they will see. So Jesus says again what he has said before (see 12:45). "Have I been with you [plural] so long, and you [singular] still do not know me, Philip?" asks Jesus. "The one who sees me has seen the Father. How can you [singular] say, 'Show us the Father'?" (14:9). And Jesus seeks again to inform what later they must see. "Do you not believe that I am in the Father and the Father is in me?" asks Jesus. "The words that I am saying to you I speak not on my own. But the Father who dwells in me does his works [ἔργα]." And Jesus points to what alone will give the eyes they need to see. "If you love me," adds Jesus, "you will heed [τηρήσετε] my instruction [ἐντολάς]."[40] And I will ask the Father. And he will give another Paraclete [ἄλλον παράκλητον]" (14:15–16).[41] He will give the Spirit of Truth (14:17).[42] For there is no knowledge of what they must know apart from the Spirit of Truth (1 Cor 12:3). There is no knowledge of the Truth in the absence of his word.

---

39. See elsewhere the only other use of ἀρκέω (suffice) also with Philip in 6:7.

40. See elsewhere τηρέω with ἐντολή in 14:21; 15:10; 1 John 2:3, 4; 3:22, 24; 5:3; and with λόγος in 8:51, 52, 55; 14:23, 24; 15:20; 17:6; 1 John 2:5. The combinations bear demonstrably equal freight. Once more, Jesus refers here not to a "commandment" or "commandments" but more broadly to the instruction of God that is light and sight to the one who believes. See further Schuchard, *1–3 John*, 151–96.

41. For Jesus as the first of these, see 1 John 2:1. See also 14:26; 15:26; 16:7. First and second work together or the work of the Father is not done. See further Köstenberger, *John*, 434–38.

42. See elsewhere "Spirit of Truth" in 15:26; 16:13; 1 John 4:6. Cf. "Spirit and Truth" in 4:23–24; and "the Spirit is the Truth" in 1 John 5:6.

Jesus will leave them soon. But he will not abandon them. "I will not leave you as orphans [ὀρφανούς],"[43] declares Jesus. "I will come to you" (14:18). He will rise and return to them. "Yet a little while and the world will see me no more," adds Jesus. "But you will see me" (14:19a). Dying, he will leave them. Rising, he will return to them. And because he lives, they also will live (14:19). For in that day they will see him as finally he must be seen. "In that day you will know that I am in my Father, and you in me, and I in you," says Jesus. And he points to the necessity of his word, saying, "The one who has [ὁ ἔχων] my instruction [ἐντολάς] and heeds [τηρῶν] it [αὐτάς], he it is who loves me" (14:20–21). It is he who will see Jesus as finally he must be seen. "And the one who loves me will be loved by my Father. And I will love him and I will disclose [ἐμφανίσω] myself to him" (14:21).[44] So the other Judas, not Iscariot, unwittingly asks, again on behalf of the others, "Lord, how is it that you will disclose yourself to us, and not to the world?" (14:22). Jesus responds, saying, "If anyone loves me, he will heed [τηρήσει] my word [λόγον]. And my Father will love him. And we will come to him and will make a [our] dwelling place [μονήν] with him" (14:23; cf. 14:2 and Rev 21:3).[45]

Again and again in their hearing as the time for Jesus's departure draws near Jesus speaks of his word that must be heard. To belong is to hear. To hear is to belong. "The one who does not love me does not heed [τηρεῖ] my words [λόγους]," declares Jesus, which are "not mine but the Father's who sent me" (14:24). To hear is everything if any are ever to see. "These things I have spoken to you[46] while I was still with you," adds Jesus (14:25). His word they have. Its necessary meaning they do not. Therefore, "the Paraclete [παράκλητος]," concludes Jesus, "the Holy Spirit,[47] whom the

---

43. See ὀρφανός (orphan) elsewhere in the New Testament only in James 1:27.

44. The verb ἐμφανίζω (disclose) appears only here in the Gospel.

45. "This is the only place in the NT where the Father and the Son are both said to indwell believers" (Köstenberger, *John*, 441).

46. The words ταῦτα λελάληκα ὑμῖν (these things I have spoken to you) appear six more times in the next two chapters. See 15:11; 16:1, 4, 6, 25, 33. See also "these things I give as instruction to you" in 15:17; "after Jesus had said these things" in 17:1; "these things I say" in 17:13; "after Jesus has said these things" in 18:1; and "after he had said these things" in 18:22, affirming the fundamental importance of what Jesus must say and they must hear if any are ever to see.

47. See elsewhere "Holy Spirit" only in 1:33; 20:22. Cf. "Holy One of God" in 6:69; and "Holy Father" in 17:11.

Father will send in my name,[48] he will teach [διδάξει] you all things and will cause you to remember [ὑπομνήσει] everything that I have said to you" (14:26).[49]

They have heard Jesus speak of his departure. They have heard him speak of his imminent return. They should have rejoiced. But they have not. Only when these things happen will the work of his hour be at an end. Then will the Spirit come (cf. 20:22). Then will they see when he imparts a peace (εἰρήνη) that is not as the world gives (14:27; see also 16:33) so they may fear no more (cf. 20:19, 21, 26). So Jesus says it again. "I have told you [all of this] before it happens," says Jesus, "so that when it does happen you may believe" (14:29). He says it all. There is little left to say. The appointed time for the accomplishment of his hour has come. The fated time for the ruler of this world to come has come (14:30). Jesus affirms his readiness for what is next. And he fatefully says, "In order that the world may know that I love the Father, and just as the Father has instructed [ἐνετείλατό][50] me, so also I do. Rise [ἐγείρεσθε]. Let us go from here" (14:31).

Whether they immediately proceed to depart is unclear. Perhaps Jesus continues to talk as they walk. Perhaps Jesus talks as they are getting ready to walk. In either case, Jesus keeps talking. He has told them that he does not have much more to say. But what he then says is as significant as ever. "I am the true [ἀληθινή] vine [ἄμπελος],"[51] declares Jesus, "[I am the embodiment of the one and only true Israel.][52] And my Father is the vinedresser [γεωργός]"[53] (15:1). For one must dress a vine to keep it

---

48. "Hence, the Father is never sent. He is sender of both the Son and the Spirit. The Spirit is never sender; he is sent by both the Father and the Son. Only Jesus is both sent one and sender; sent by the Father, he sends both the Spirit and the disciples" (Köstenberger, *John*, 442).

49. See also the Paraclete as Teacher in 1 John 2:20, 27. "The Spirit will not provide qualitatively new or independent revelation," observes Köstenberger, *John*, 442. Neither does Jesus (see esp. 7:16). The Spirit brings to light "the true meaning and significance of the revelation imparted by Jesus."

50. Cf. 15:14, 17.

51. The vocable ἄμπελος (vine) appears elsewhere in the New Testament only in Matthew 26:29 (and its parallels); James 3:12; Revelation 14:18–19.

52. See Köstenberger, *John*, 448–50.

53. The vocable γεωργός (vinedresser) appears elsewhere in the New Testament only in Matthew 21:33–41 (and its parallels); 2 Timothy 2:6; James 5:7. Cf. Noah in LXX Genesis 9:20; Issachar in LXX Genesis 49:14–15; and LXX Jeremiah 38:24.

healthy. "Every branch [κλῆμα]⁵⁴ in me that does not bear fruit [καρπόν]⁵⁵ he takes away," adds Jesus, "and every branch that does bear fruit he cleanses [prunes] [καθαίρει],⁵⁶ so that it may bear [even] more fruit" (15:2). What is dead and dying is taken away. Only what lives remains. It remains so it may thrive.

"You are already clean [καθαροί],"⁵⁷ declares Jesus, "on account of the word that I have spoken to you" (15:3). They are living, fruit-bearing branches. For they have believed what he has said. And so they are what he has said. But a greater, final pruning must reckon once and for all with every last vestige of what is dead and dying. For this reason, especially in light of what is to come, Jesus urges his disciples again to heed what he has said.⁵⁸ He urges them to love as he has loved. For just so will he love (15:4–12). Just so will he show the full extent of his love (13:1). For "greater love has no one than this," declares Jesus, "that one lays down his life for his loved ones" (15:13).⁵⁹ What Jesus does they too will do when he transformatively loves. What Jesus does they will do when he and his cruciform example—when he and his cruciform word—are the reason that they see.

"No longer do I call you servants [δούλους]," declares Jesus. "For the servant does not know what his master is doing [cf. 13:16]. Instead, I have called you loved ones [φίλους]. For everything that I have heard from my Father I have made known to you" (15:15). "These things I give as

---

54. "Branch" (κλῆμα) appears elsewhere in the New Testament only in 15:4–6. Cf. LXX Psalm 79:1–12 (esp. v. 1); Joel 1:7; Nahum 2:3; Malachi 3:19; Ezekiel 17:1–24 (esp. vv. 5–8, 22–23); 19:1–14 (esp. vv. 10–11).

55. Outside 15:1–16, where καρπός (fruit) appears eight times, see the fruit-bearing in 4:36 and 12:24.

56. The verb καθαίρω (make clean, clear, prune) appears only here in the New Testament. In the LXX, it appears only in 2 Samuel 4:6; Isaiah 28:7. Cf. καθαροί (clean) in 15:3.

57. Cf. καθαίρω (make clean, clear, prune) in 15:2. The vocable καθαρός (clean) appears elsewhere in the Gospel only in 13:10–11, where Jesus likewise says, "You are clean, but not all of you." See also καθαρισμός (cleansing) in 2:6.

58. See especially ἐὰν τὰς ἐντολάς μου τηρήσητε (if you heed my instruction) in 15:10; and αὕτη ἐστὶν ἡ ἐντολὴ ἡ ἐμή (this is my instruction) in 15:12. Cf. εἰ τὸν λόγον μου ἐτήρησαν (if they heed my word) in 15:20. Again, ἐντολή refers here not to a "commandment" or "commandments" but more broadly to the instruction of God that is light and sight to the person who believes. See further Schuchard, *1–3 John*, 151–96.

59. Outside 15:13–15, the φίλοι (loved ones) of Jesus are John (3:29) and Lazarus (11:11). See also 3 John 15. Contrast the negative characterization of Pilate in 19:12. See further the ancient world's esteem for φίλοι in Köstenberger, *John*, 458–59.

instruction [ἐντέλλομαι] to you," adds Jesus, "so you will love one another" (15:17). Once more, Jesus underscores the necessity of his word, from him to them and from them to the rest of the world. "Remember the word that I have spoken to you," declares Jesus. "If they heed [ἐτήρησαν] my word, they will heed [τηρήσουσιν] yours also" (15:20). For the disciple's word will be his word. As he has before, Jesus underscores the complementary necessity of the Spirit of Truth. For the Spirit of Truth must likewise come to disclose all truth through the remembrance of Jesus's word. The Spirit must come, or none can know the Truth. So Jesus says it again: "When the Paraclete comes, whom I will send to you from the Father, the Spirit of Truth, who proceeds from the Father, he will testify about me. And you too will testify, because you have been with me from the beginning"[60] (15:26–27). They too will testify. They too will be the enduring reality of his living, life-giving voice. They too will be this and do this because they have been with him. They have been with him so they would hear and believe and be these things.

"I have said these things to you," declares Jesus, "so [what happens next] will not shock you [σκανδαλισθῆτε]" (16:1). Sadly, he says this, knowing that it will.[61] The apparent death wish of their master will alarm them. His inexplicable determination to go the way of the cross will distress them. His resolve in the face of his betrayal will dumbfound them. His arrest will send them into a panic. They will scatter. They will flee. From a distance, they will look to see what becomes of him. They will watch as he suffers and dies. His extraordinary suffering will horrify. His ignominious death will devastate. They will grievously mourn. They will fear. They will be terrified. They will cower. They will wonder. Were they just wrong about him? Were they somehow deceived? Was it all a hoax? How could they have been so wrong? What is to become of them now? Knowing this is what they will do, knowing this is what they will think, Jesus acts to prevent it from being what ultimately defines them. Instead, he prepares them for what is next. Jesus tells them what they must remember. He preps them for the time when they too will speak a word that must be heard.

---

60. See elsewhere ἀπ᾽ ἀρχῆς (from the beginning) only in 8:44. Cf. "in the beginning" (ἐν ἀρχῇ) only in 1:1–2; and "from the beginning" (ἐξ ἀρχῆς) only in 6:64; 16:4.

61. Cf. "You will all be shocked [σκανδαλισθήσεσθε] by me this night" in Matthew 26:31. See also Mark 14:27.

"An hour [ὥρα] is coming [ἔρχεται],"⁶² says Jesus, "when whoever kills you will think that he is offering service [λατρείαν]⁶³ to God" (16:2).⁶⁴ "I have said these things to you," adds Jesus, "so when their hour comes you may remember that I told them to you" (16:4). Jesus says these things so they too will say the same things. He intends to encourage. But his words trigger an opposite reaction. Grief (λύπη)⁶⁵ fills their hearts (16:6). And so, once more, he who is the Truth tells them the truth or they will never see.

"It is better for you that I go away," declares Jesus. "For if I do not go away, the Paraclete will not come to you.⁶⁶ But if I go I will send him to you. When he comes, that one will convict [ἐλέγξει]⁶⁷ the world concerning [περί] sin [ἁμαρτίας]⁶⁸ and concerning righteousness [δικαιοσύνης]⁶⁹ and concerning judgment [κρίσεως]"⁷⁰ (16:7–8). "I still have many things [that I would like] to say to you," adds Jesus, "but you are not able to bear [them] now. When that one comes, the Spirit of Truth, he will guide [ὁδηγήσει]⁷¹ you in all truth. For he will not speak on his own. Instead, whatever he hears he will speak, and he will proclaim to you the things that are to come. That one will glorify me. For he will take from me

62. See elsewhere ἔρχεται ὥρα (an hour is coming) in 4:21, 23; 5:25, 28; 16:25, 32. See also the references to his hour that "has come" in 12:23 (cf. "I have come to this hour" in 12:27); 16:32; 17:1; "is now" in 4:23; 5:25; "had come" in 13:1. Contrast "has not yet come" in 2:4; "had not yet come" in 7:30; 8:20; "because her hour has come" in 16:21; "when their hour comes" in 16:4; "from that hour" in 19:27.

63. The vocable λατρείαν (service, worship) appears elsewhere in the New Testament only in Romans 9:4; 12:1; Hebrews 9:1, 6. The cognate verb λατρεύω is far more frequent, but is not used by John either in his Gospel or in his epistles. See, however, Revelation 7:15; 22:3.

64. "The statement probably refers to Jewish rather than Roman persecution," observes Köstenberger, *John*, 469. "In his pre-Christian days, Paul certainly reflected such misguided zeal for his ancestral traditions (see Acts 8:1–3; 26:9–12; Gal. 1:13–14). Later Paul suffered similar persecution at the hands of others (2 Cor. 11:24)." Cf. above Israel's misguided zeal in 2:17; and "if they persecuted me, they will also persecute you" (15:20).

65. See elsewhere λύπη (grief) only in 16:20–22.

66. Köstenberger, *John*, 471, observes rightly that "OT prophetic literature is full of anticipation regarding the inauguration of the age of the kingdom of God by the pouring out of the Holy Spirit." See Isaiah 11:1–10; 32:14–18; 42:1–4; 44:1–5; Jeremiah 31:31–34; Ezekiel 11:17–20; 36:24–27; 37:1–14; Joel 2:28–32.

67. See elsewhere ἐλέγχω (convict, reprove, expose) only in 3:20; 8:46.

68. See elsewhere ἁμαρτία (sin) in 1:29; 8:21, 24, 34, 46; 9:34, 41; 15:22, 24; 16:9; 19:11; 20:23. See also ἁμαρτωλός (sinful) in 9:16, 24, 25, 31; and the verb ἁμαρτάνω (sin) in 5:14; 8:11; 9:2, 3.

69. See elsewhere δικαιοσύνη (righteousness) only in 16:10. See also δίκαιος (righteous) in 5:30; 7:24; 17:25.

70. See elsewhere κρίσις (judgment) in 3:19; 5:22, 24, 27, 29, 30; 7:24; 8:16; 12:31; 16:11. See also the verb κρίνω (judge) in 3:17, 18; 5:22, 30; 7:24, 51; 8:15, 16, 26, 50; 12:47, 48; 16:11; 18:31.

71. The vocable ὁδηγέω (lead [the way], guide) appears only here.

and proclaim [it] to you. Everything that the Father has is mine. For
this reason I said that he will take from me and proclaim [it] to you"
(16:12–15).[72] He speaks again of his death as departure, but promises again
to return to them soon.[73] "In a little while [μιχρόν], you will see me no
longer," declares Jesus. "In a little while, you will see me again" (16:16). In
a little while, he will die. In a little while, he will rise and return to them.
But because the Spirit has not yet come (7:39) they fail to comprehend
his words (16:17). Instead, they poignantly say, "We do not know what
he is talking about" (16:18).

Again, Jesus knows that his words are too much for them now (16:19).
But a day will soon come when clarity will finally come. So he urges them
all to await that day. "You will weep [κλαύσετε] and lament [θρηνήσετε],"
declares Jesus, "but the world will rejoice [χαρήσεται]. You will grieve
[λυπηθήσεσθε],[74] but your grief will turn into joy" (16:20).[75] "I will see
you again," adds Jesus. "And your hearts will rejoice, and no one will take
your joy from you" (16:22). "I have said these things to you in figures
[παροιμίαις]" (16:25a; cf. 10:6), explains Jesus. He speaks in anticipation
of the arrival and the accomplishment of his hour. But foresight fails them.
With the arrival and the accomplishment of his hour what the Spirit will
give is twenty-twenty hindsight.

"The hour is coming," pledges Jesus, "when I will no longer speak to
you in figures. Instead, I will tell you [everything] openly." He will speak
directly. He will leave nothing out (16:25). "I have come from the Father
and have come into the world," declares Jesus. "Even now I am leaving the
world and going to the Father" (16:28).[76] His disciples unwittingly imagine

---

72. Thus, only when the Spirit of Truth illumines the way by means of the word of the Word
Made Flesh will they finally see Jesus, who is the Way, the Truth, and the Life (14:4–6; see also 1:23),
as finally he must be seen.

73. See Carson, *John*, 543. See also Köstenberger, *John*, 474–75. Cf. μιχρόν (a little while) twice
modifying χρόνον (referring to an indefinite period of "time") in 7:33 and 12:35; and standing alone
in 13:33; 14:19; and in 16:16–19 (where μιχρόν appears seven times!).

74. See elsewhere λυπέω (grieve) only in 21:17.

75. See further the analogy of the woman in the anguish of labor (16:20–22) in Bruce G.
Schuchard, "The Wedding Feast at Cana and the Christological Monomania of St. John," in *All
Theology is Christology: Essays in Honor of David P. Scaer*, ed. Dean O. Wenthe et al. (Fort Wayne, IN:
Concordia Theological Seminary Press, 2000), 110n31. For additional background, see Köstenberger,
John, 476.

76. Cf. Jesus's return to his Father in 7:33; 13:1; 14:12, 28.

that Jesus is already speaking to them in plain terms. But he is not. What it means for Jesus to have come from God they do not see. Neither are they seeing what it will mean for Jesus to go to God. Instead, they mistakenly say, "Behold, now you are speaking openly. Now you are speaking without using figures" (16:29). They could not be more mistaken.[77] They are and for now will remain ignorant of what "coming from" or "going to" means. And so, once more, they ironically speak a truth that is greater than they can possibly know. And they say, "For this reason, we believe that you have come from God" (16:30b).

"Really?" asks Jesus. "Do you now believe?" (16:31). Do they now see? "Behold, the hour [ὥρα] is coming," declares Jesus, "indeed it has come, when you will be scattered,[78] each [of you] to the persons and things of his own home [εἰς τὰ ἴδια].[79] And you will leave me alone. Yet I am not alone, for the Father is with me" (16:32). They see but do not see, not yet. Only Jesus knows who he really is. Only Jesus sees what soon must be. He sees that the day is fast approaching when they too will finally see. He sees what they must hear so that later they may see. And so Jesus says, "I have said these things to you, so in me you may have peace [εἰρήνην]" (16:33a; cf. 14:27).[80] When the time is right and the deed is done, they will see him again. And his peace will be their peace, like no other peace. For his is a peace that makes all things new. His is a peace that makes all things right when with it comes understanding. "In the world you will have tribulation [θλῖψιν]" (cf. 16:21), adds Jesus. "But take heart, I have overcome [νενίκηκα] the world" (16:33b).[81] And in their hearing Jesus

---

77. Thus, Köstenberger rightly finds here "another glaring and climactic instance of Johannine misunderstanding." Their "claim to clarity is as enthusiastic as it is impetuous." Despite their confidence, "the disciples are no closer to understanding than before" (*John*, 479).

78. Cf. "and the wolf snatches them and scatters them" in 10:12. See also "strike the shepherd, and the sheep will be scattered" (Zech 13:7).

79. Failing to see in the arrival of his hour that they are his own (cf. εἰς τὰ ἴδια in 1:11) for whom he has come to suffer and die (see also "and the disciple took her εἰς τὰ ἴδια" in 19:27), they all will be scattered, each to what otherwise remains as is his own. See further ἴδιος in 1:41; 4:44; 5:18, 43; 7:18; 8:44; 10:3, 4, 12; 13:1; 15:19.

80. "Jesus looks beyond their defection to their restoration and promises them peace (cf. 14:27)" (Köstenberger, *John*, 480). See further 20:19, 21, 26. Thus, as it should, "the farewell discourse proper ends on a triumphant note" (480–81).

81. Cf. the theme of triumph in 1 John 2:13, 14; 4:4; 5:4–5. The theme is especially prevalent in Revelation.

prays to his Father.[82] For himself Jesus need not say a word. For he is the Word Made Flesh. Jesus prays, then, not for his sake but for their sake. He prays so by the Spirit of Truth the truth of him who is the Truth will be what they finally see.[83]

"Father," declares Jesus, "the hour [ὥρα] has come. Glorify your Son that the Son may glorify you" (17:1; cf. 12:23, 28). For all authority has been given to Jesus to impart to all flesh the life of the age to come (17:2). He is the only way. And so Jesus says, "This is the life of the age to come." This is what the disciples must know. "They [must] know you," declares Jesus, "the only [μόνον] true [ἀληθινόν] God [θεόν],"[84] and "Jesus Christ[85] whom you have sent" (17:3). For the knowledge of the one (of Jesus) is the knowledge of the other. Just as there is but one true God, there is but one way to know the true God.[86] Christ alone makes God known (1:18; 14:6–11). And so Jesus says, "I have manifested [ἐφανέρωσά][87] your name [ὄνομα] to the people [ἀνθρώποις] that you gave me out of the world. Yours they were, and you gave them to me, and they have heeded [τετήρηκαν] your word"[88] (17:6). For the word of the Father is the word of Jesus, the word of the Word Made Flesh.[89] Witting or not, the disciples have embraced Jesus's word. They will do so especially two days hence when his words inform and his form is seen as that of the God that must be seen (14:9).

---

82. "The prayer is often called Jesus' 'high-priestly prayer' (a designation reaching back at least as far as the sixteenth century), though this label hardly fits with Johannine thought, which does not picture Jesus as a high priest" (Köstenberger, *John*, 482). See further Carson, *John*, 552–53; and Ridderbos, *John*, 546.

83. For what follows, see further Bruce G. Schuchard, "'That They May Be One': Lutheran Interpretation of John 17 from the Reformation to Today," in *Lutheran Catholicity*, ed. John A. Maxfield, The Pieper Lectures 5 (St. Louis: Concordia Historical Institute and the Luther Academy, 2001), 83–98.

84. Cf. "the glory that comes from the only God," 5:44; "the one who sent me is true [ἀληθινός]," 7:28; and "we know that the Son of God has come and has given us understanding, so that we may know the one who is true [τὸν ἀληθινόν], and we are in the one who is true [τῷ ἀληθινῷ], in his Son, Jesus Christ," 1 John 5:20.

85. The designation "Jesus Christ" appears elsewhere only in 1:17. Jesus's remarkable manner of referring to himself may well signal "the extent to which Jesus from the beginning involved the overhearing disciples in his prayer by once more depicting before their eyes the power given him by the Father in its full salvific meaning, as it concerned them" (Ridderbos, *John*, 549). Cf. "that you may believe that Jesus is the Christ," 20:31.

86. Köstenberger, *John*, 489.

87. Cf. 2:11; 21:1, 14.

88. Cf. 8:51, 52, 55; 14:23, 24; 15:20.

89. Cf. "and the word that you hear is not mine but the Father's who sent me" in 14:24.

"They know that everything that you have given me is from you," declares Jesus. "For I have given them the words that you gave me.⁹⁰ And they have received them and have truly come to know that I have come from you" (17:7–8).⁹¹ "But now I am coming to you," adds Jesus, "and these things I speak in the world so they may have my joy fulfilled in themselves" (17:13). His joy will be their joy when the time comes and they remember what they have heard. "I have given them your word," concludes Jesus. "I do not ask that you take them out of the world, but that you preserve [τηρήσῃς] them from the evil one"⁹² (17:14–15). And Jesus petitions his Father for the one thing that will ensure their safety. "Sanctify them in the truth," declares Jesus. "Your word is truth" (17:17; cf. 1:14, 17; 14:6), says he who is the Truth that they must finally see (17:24).

Then Jesus and his disciples cross the Kidron and enter a garden (κῆπος)⁹³ on the other side (18:1). Judas knows of the place, for it is where Jesus and his disciples have often met (18:2). So the betrayer (ὁ παραδιδούς, 18:2) comes with a band of soldiers and officers from the chief priests and the Pharisees (18:3). But Jesus knows that they are coming (18:4), so he takes the initiative, and he goes to them and asks, "Whom do you seek?" (cf. 1:38; 20:15). They answer, saying, "Jesus, the Nazarene [τὸν Ναζωραῖον]" (cf. 19:19; see also 1:45–46). Jesus responds, saying, "I am [he] [ἐγώ εἰμι]" (18:5).⁹⁴ Now in John's story of Jesus, either one turns/comes toward Jesus and lives or one turns/goes away from him and dies. And so, in response to the word of the Word Made Flesh, Judas and those with him turn/go away (ἀπῆλθον εἰς τὰ ὀπίσω)⁹⁵ and fall

---

90. Cf. "And I will put my words in his mouth, and he will speak to them as I instruct him" in LXX Deuteronomy 18:18; and Jesus who does only what the Father has instructed him to do in 14:31.

91. Like a "solemn refrain," the phrase ὅτι σύ με ἀπέστειλας (that you sent me), first appearing in 11:42, recurs here and in 17:21, 23, 25 (Köstenberger, *John*, 492). Cf. the fundamental importance of knowing the one whom the Father has sent in 17:3; "just as you have sent me into the world so also have I sent them into the world" in 17:18; and "just as the Father has sent me so also am I sending you" in 20:21.

92. Cf. 6:70; 8:44; 12:31; 13:2, 27; 14:30; 16:11.

93. See also 18:26; 19:41. Thus, the narrative of the betrayal, arrest, trial, crucifixion, death, and burial of Jesus begins and ends in a garden.

94. Compare and contrast ἐγώ εἰμι (I am [he]) (18:5, 6, 8) with Peter, who says, "I am not" (18:17, 25, 27).

95. Cf. those who turn/go away from Jesus (ἀπῆλθον εἰς τὰ ὀπίσω) in 6:66; toward Jesus (ἴδε ὁ κόσμος ὀπίσω αὐτοῦ ἀπῆλθεν) in 12:19; and toward Jesus (ἐστράφη εἰς τὰ ὀπίσω) in 20:14 (see also 20:16).

to the ground (καὶ ἔπεσαν χαμαι)[96] (18:6). They fall as will all who refuse what they must hear.[97]

Jesus asks again, "Whom do you seek?" In spite of what has just happened, they offer the same answer (18:7). What is not said is whether the same answer was given while the representatives of the seemingly invincible power of Rome and those of Israel's elite still lay on the ground. In either case, their answer is the same. Thus, their seeking is a tragically persistent one that malevolently turns not toward and for but against the Word Made Flesh (cf. 1:11). Yet the moment is ironically also the very hour for which Jesus has come (17:1). "I told you that I am [he] [ἐγώ εἰμι]," responds Jesus. "So if you seek me, let these [men] go" (18:8). Thus, the Savior acts to preserve those who are his own even as he also shows that he alone is powerful to determine the course of what follows. For the path that has been set is for him and him alone (8:21; 13:33, 36). Only he can go where he must go. Only he can do what he must do. Therefore, Jesus embraces what he must do and says to an unwitting Peter in the hearing of all the rest, "Shall I not drink the cup [ποτήριον] that the Father has given me?" (18:10–11).[98] So they seize Jesus, bind him (cf. 11:44; 18:24; 19:40), and take him first to Annas, the father-in-law of Caiaphas (18:12–13; cf. Luke 3:2; Acts 4:6).[99]

Simon Peter and the Beloved Disciple follow (18:15).[100] Because the Beloved Disciple is known to the high priest,[101] he enters with Jesus into the dwelling (αὐλή; cf. elsewhere only in 10:1, 16) of the high priest.[102]

---

96. Contrast falling at Jesus's feet in 11:32 with falling to the earth and dying in 12:24. The verb πίπτω (fall) appears frequently in Revelation. See esp. falling down "as though dead" in Revelation 1:17. The adverb χαμαί (to the ground) appears elsewhere only in 9:6.

97. Cf. the fate of those who refuse to hear in LXX Psalm 9:4; 34:4; 39:15; 55:10; 69:3; 77:66; 113:3, 5; 128:5. See also the serpent Dan in Genesis 49:17; and the consequence of Israel's persistent refusal to hear in Isaiah 28:13; 42:17.

98. Jesus speaks of the cup of the Father's wrath (see LXX Ps 74:9; Isa 51:17, 22; Jer 32:15, 17, 28; Lam 2:13; Ezek 23:31–33. See also Rev 16:19). From it Jesus drinks (see Matt 22:22–23; 26:39; Mark 10:38–39; 14:36; Luke 22:42), so that the cup of salvation that results (LXX Ps 115:4) may then be his to give. See Matthew 26:27; Mark 14:23; Luke 22:20; 1 Corinthians 10:16, 21, 25–27.

99. For the history and relationship of Annas and Caiaphas, see further Köstenberger, *John*, 512–13, 515–18.

100. For the identity here of the anonymous disciple, see Köstenberger, *John*, 513, and those that Köstenberger cites.

101. See further Köstenberger, *John*, 513–14.

102. See also the αὐλή of the temple in Revelation 11:2.

Inside, the Beloved Disciple speaks with the doorkeeper (θυρωρός; cf. elsewhere only in 10:3) at the door (θύρα; cf. 10:1, 2, 7, 9; see further below 20:19, 26) and leads Peter in (18:16).[103] First, Annas questions Jesus. Then Caiaphas asks even more questions (18:24). The spectacle is "highly ironic."[104] Jesus suggests in his trial that those who have heard him speak can attest to what he has said (18:20). But, when challenged, Peter steadfastly declares that he knows nothing. Then they take Jesus to Pilate.[105] At the praetorium, those who bring Jesus do not enter. Instead, they ironically stay outside because they do not wish to defile themselves (18:28). And yet they otherwise defile themselves in every way as they resort to extraordinary measures to seek the death of an innocent man. They stay outside in the hope that what they still are determined to do does not prevent them from having the time that they need to eat the Passover[106] before sunrise (see Exod 12:10).[107] Jesus goes inside. And Pilate comes outside to speak with those who are there (18:29).

First Pilate calls into question whether their problem is something that requires his attention. "Take him and judge him by your own law," says

---

103. The θυρωρός (doorkeeper) at the θύρα (door) of the αὐλή (dwelling place) of the high priest in 18:16–17 recalls the θυρωρός at the θύρα of the αὐλή in 10:3. For Mark W. G. Stibbe, this may well "explain why John 10 has this otherwise unnecessary detail" (*John as Storyteller: Narrative Criticism and the Fourth Gospel*, SNTSMS 73 [Cambridge: Cambridge University Press, 1992], 103). See further κλέπτης (thief) in 10:1, 8, 10 and in 12:4–6 and nowhere else (see also Judas in 13:2, 10–11, 26–30; 18:2–6); λῃστής (robber) in 10:1, 8, and in 18:40 and nowhere else; the one who calls his own by name in 10:3 and in 11:43 and 20:16; "follow" (ἀκολουθέω) in 10:4, 27 and in 11:31; 12:26; 13:36–37; 18:15; 20:6; 21:19, 20, 22; the hired hand who leaves the sheep because "he cares not" concerning the sheep and the wolf who then seizes and scatters in 10:12–13 and in 12:6 and in 16:32, where Jesus says to his disciples, "you will be scattered and leave me alone"; the Good Shepherd who lays down his life for the sheep and takes it up again in 10:11, 14–18, and in 13:4, 12, where Jesus lays down and takes up his garments (cf. "I will lay down my life for you" in 13:37–38) and in 15:13 where Jesus declares, "greater love has no one than this, that one lays down his life for his loved ones"; and "other sheep that are not of this dwelling place" in 10:16 and in 12:20–23, where certain Greeks wish to see Jesus. Thus, what Jesus consistently foreshadows in John 10 takes ever greater final shape and form with the arrival and the accomplishment of his hour that follows.

104. Stibbe, *John as Storyteller*, 97.

105. Ironically, it is especially the chief priests who take the Lamb (1:29, 36; cf. temple in 2:19–21) to Pilate. See 18:35; 19:6, 15, 21. Later, it is especially they who interact with Pilate. See further their malevolence in 7:32, 45; 11:47, 49, 51, 57; 12:10; 18:3, 10, 13, 15, 16, 19, 22, 24, 26.

106. Cf. the eating of the Bread of Life in 6:26–59.

107. According to Exodus 12:10, they have until the sun rises to eat the Passover. For πρωΐ (early) in 18:28 as a reference to the fourth watch of the night (from roughly three in the morning to six in the morning), see BDAG, s.v. πρωΐ. See further on the only other use of πρωΐ in 20:1 with reference to a time when it was "still dark."

Pilate (18:31a). But they insist that Pilate's response is required because Jesus is guilty of a capital crime. Ironically, they say not with reference to their law but to Roman law, "We are not permitted to kill anyone" (18:31b). Their charge is that Jesus claims to be king. The charge is significant both to them and to Rome, but for different reasons. If guilty, and Pilate judges the case, the verdict will be a usual one. Jesus will be crucified. Thus, those bringing charges against Jesus seek more than his death. They want his name to be heaped in shame. They want him to be forgotten. "Crucify!" will be what they cry (19:6).

The previous word of Jesus by which he signified (σημαίνων) the sort of death that he was going to die (12:33) sees its fulfilment (18:32).[108] Pilate goes inside, summons Jesus, and asks, "Are you the king of the Jews?" (18:33). Jesus responds in the affirmative (18:36) but is also quick to observe that his is a kingdom that is not of this world.[109] "For this purpose I was born [γεγέννημαι]," declares Jesus.[110] For this purpose Jesus has come, not to rise up in revolt against Rome but to bear witness to the truth. "Everyone who is of the truth," declares Jesus, "hears my voice" (18:37). Thus, the kingdom in which Jesus reigns is one in which the Truth that is Jesus is everything. One hears the word of the Word Made Flesh and belongs to the kingdom in which he is King, or never will one see (3:3).

Pilate finds amusing Jesus's suggestion that his kingdom is a realm where the Truth that Jesus is defines all things. So Pilate ironically asks, "What is truth?" (18:38a).[111] Who is to say? Why should the truth of which Jesus speaks be more significant than any other truth? No doubt irked by the seemingly trivial nature of the threat posed by this itinerant Jew, Pilate goes out to those who are still outside, and he speaks a truth that is greater than he can possibly know. "I find in him no cause [for legal action],"

---

108. Thus, both the verb σημαίνω ("signify" in 12:33 and 18:32; see also 21:19) and its cognate σημεῖον ("sign," appearing in the Gospel seventeen times) regularly *signify* beforehand the fundamental importance and eschatological meaning of the death that Jesus has come to die.

109. See elsewhere βασιλεία (kingdom) only in 3:3, 5.

110. Only here does the Gospel refer to his birth.

111. That Pilate likely responds from a "political, pragmatic point of view" is suggested by Köstenberger, *John*, 529. That his response is cynical is suggested by Carson, *John*, 595. For Ben Witherington III, "Pilate concludes that Jesus is a deluded quack whom he can banter with but not take seriously" (*John's Wisdom: A Commentary on the Fourth Gospel* [Louisville: Westminster John Knox, 1995], 292).

declares Pilate (18:38b).[112] Jesus is innocent. So Pilate tries to release him (18:39). But Jesus's accusers are determined to see him dead. So they add to what they have already said. This time with reference to their own law, they ironically say, "We have a law. And according to that law he ought to die because he has claimed that he is the Son of God" (19:7).

Pilate ironically fears "the prospect of confrontation with the supernatural"[113] (19:8). So he returns to Jesus and ironically asks him, "Where do you come from?" (19:9). But Jesus refuses to answer. "Do you not know," asks Pilate, "that I have authority to release you and I have authority to crucify you? (19:10). But the authority to determine what happens next is that of heaven above (19:11). So Jesus says nothing. Pilate tries again to release him. But, again, those accusing Jesus act quickly to prevent his release. To Pilate they say, "If you release this man, you are no friend [φίλος] of Caesar." This Jesus claims that he is the Son of God. He claims that he is king. And so they cunningly say, "Every individual who makes himself king opposes Caesar" (19:12). Pilate sees the genuine threat that their challenge now poses to him if Pilate releases Jesus. So Pilate acquiesces. Before doing so, however, Pilate challenges Jesus's accusers to offer a clear indication of their own fealty to Caesar. Speaking again a truth that is greater than any of them can possibly know, Pilate points to Jesus and says, "Behold your king!" (19:14). Sadly, they respond as Pilate expects with the deeply unsettling and astonishingly tragic, "We have no king but Caesar" (19:15).[114]

---

112. "The case against Jesus is groundless," observes Köstenberger, *John*, 502. Pilate states three times that he finds no legal basis for the charges they have brought against Jesus (18:38; 19:4, 6).

113. Craig R. Koester, *Symbolism in the Fourth Gospel: Meaning, Mystery, Community*, 2nd ed. (Minneapolis: Fortress, 2003), 215. To pagan ears, "the designation 'son of god' conjured up notions of 'divine men,' persons believed to enjoy certain divine powers" (Köstenberger, *John*, 534). Many of Rome's emperors claimed to be Son of God. Domitian required that all his subjects hail him not only as Son of God but also as "Lord and God," see Köstenberger, *John*, 579–80. See "my Lord and my God" in 20:29.

114. "The Passover meal celebrated God's victory over Pharaoh," observes Koester, *Symbolism*, 216 (citing Meeks and Duke). "During the meal God's sole sovereignty was praised with words like, 'From everlasting you are God. ... We have no king but you.' " See further the "unprincipled alliance" of Rome's governor and the Jews in Ridderbos, *John*, 586–87, who aptly notes the trial narrative's masterful way of suggesting "that the deep hostility between Pilate and the Jews did not prevent them from finally uniting into a single front against Jesus. Both parties had to do violence to their own positions—Pilate by allowing himself to be blackmailed as 'a friend of the emperor' by the despised Jews, the Jews by passing themselves off to him as those who recognized no other king than the emperor and therefore wanted nothing to do with a 'king of the Jews.' "

It is the sixth hour of the sixth day of the week (19:14). It is the Day of Preparation (παρασκευή). For *every* sixth day of an Israelite week was a day of preparation. Every sixth day was the Day of Preparation for the Sabbath.[115] But the day is also an exceptional day. The day is the sixth day of the Gospel's third and final Passover (12:1), of its sixth and final feast.[116] For the time has come for the Lamb of God to take away the sin of the world (1:29). His sacrifice will end all sacrifice. His Passover will end all Passovers. Pilate composes an inscription to affix it to the cross. Intended as a declaration of Jesus's guilt, the inscription speaks instead a truth that is greater than any of them can possibly know. Written in Aramaic, Latin, and Greek, the inscription reads, "Jesus, the Nazarene, the King of the Jews" (19:19–20). Israel's chief priests object, wishing that Pilate had written instead that Jesus had claimed falsely that he was king (19:21). Fittingly, Pilate refuses to alter what he has done and ironically states, "What I have written [ὃ γέγραφα] I have written [γέγραφα]" (19:22).

Present at the crucifixion of Jesus are four men, four Gentile soldiers (19:23), and four Jewish women (19:25). The Beloved Disciple is also there (19:26–27). Tellingly, they all receive something from the one on the cross.[117] The men, the soldiers, receive Jesus's garments (ἱμάτια) (19:23–24), including his tunic (χιτνών). The tunic is woven (ὑφαντός) and seamless

---

115. For this reason, the day is called the προσάββατον (day before the Sabbath) in Mark 15:42.

116. From the tenth of Nisan to the fifteenth of Nisan is six days. See above the analysis of "six days before the Passover" in 12:1. See also the Gospel's first Passover in 2:13, 23; its second in 6:4; and its first reference to the approach of the Gospel's third and final Passover in 11:55. See further the unnamed feast in 5:1; Tabernacles in 7:2; and the Feast of the Dedication in 10:22. See finally the Gospel's third and final Passover, in 13:1; 18:28, 39; 19:14. In 19:14, the genitive τοῦ πάσχα in the phrase παρασκευὴ τοῦ πάσχα (Day of Preparation *of* the Passover) is then a genitive of apposition. Thus, 19:14 refers not to a "day of preparation *for* the Passover" (never was the Day of Preparation a day to prepare for anything other than the Sabbath), but to a "Day of Preparation [for the Sabbath] *that was* the Passover." For the sixth hour as a reference to six in the morning, see Witherington, *John's Wisdom*, 294. See also Brooke F. Westcott, *The Gospel according to St. John: The Authorized Version with Introduction and Notes* (repr., Grand Rapids: Eerdmans, 1981), 282, and the sources that he cites; and Armand J. Gagne Jr., "An Examination and Possible Explanation of John's Dating of the Crucifixion," in *The Death of Jesus in the Fourth Gospel*, ed. Gilbert Van Belle, BETL 200 (Leuven: Leuven University Press, 2007), 420.

117. The total is, then, five persons of Jewish descent. For what follows, see further Bruce G. Schuchard, *Scripture within Scripture: The Interrelationship of Form and Function in the Explicit Old Testament Citations in the Gospel of John*, SBLDS 133 (Atlanta: Scholars Press, 1992), 125–32.

(ἄραφος), as is the temple veil.[118] For the time has come for Jesus as Temple, as place of the glory and of sacrifice, to become the sacrifice to end all sacrifice. In the company of the Beloved Disciple, the women receive also. They receive an emblematic indication of what Jesus's work will mean for those who are of his house (8:35; 14:2). Jesus entrusts his mother to the care of the disciple (19:26–27).[119] For the future responsibility of caring for Jesus's house (8:35; 14:2–3)[120] is to be that of his sent ones (20:21–23).[121] In the stead of Jesus (see "behold your son" in 19:26) and by his command (see "behold your mother" in 19:27), Jesus's sent ones will serve from this time forward in the gathering (21:1–14) and the care of the sheep of the Good Shepherd (21:15–17). They will care for them all, both Jew and Gentile, until Jesus comes again.

Jesus knows that his end is nigh (cf. 13:1). And so he declares, "I thirst!" (19:28). He from whom rivers of living water will soon flow thirsts so that all who thirst may thirst no more (6:35).[122] The Mouth of God receives with his mouth the bitter (19:29)[123] so that his loved ones may receive with

---

118. See ὑφαντός in LXX Exodus 26:31.

119. See his words to her: "Woman, behold your son [υἱός]" (19:26); and to him: "Behold, your mother [μήτηρ]" (19:27). Similarly, Mary L. Coloe (citing others), offers the complementary suggestion that "only in this Gospel is Jesus arrested and buried in a garden (18:1; 19:41)." In the midst of that which thus frames the passion Jesus is himself crucified "in the midst" (19:18; see also 1:26; 20:19, 26), echoing the use of the phrase in Genesis 2:9, where God likewise places the tree of life "in the midst" of the garden. Thus, "the evangelist depicts the crucifixion with the iconography of Genesis 2: there is a garden, and in the middle of the garden is the cross, the tree of life, and at the foot of the cross stand a man, the Beloved Disciple, and a woman, who is never named but called only 'Woman' (John 2:4; 19:26) and 'Mother' (2:1; 19:25), echoing the names given to the first woman (Gen 2:23; 3:20)," "The Mother of Jesus: A Woman Possessed," in *Character Studies in the Fourth Gospel: Narrative Approaches to Seventy Figures in John*, eds. Steven A. Hunt et al. (Grand Rapids: Eerdmans, 2013), 211.

120. See the *true* mother and brothers and sisters of Jesus in Matthew 12:46–50; Mark 3:21, 31–35; Luke 8:19–21.

121. See Andrew T. Lincoln, *The Gospel according to John*, BNTC 4 (New York: Continuum, 2005), 476–77. See further Nicolas Farelly, *The Disciples in the Fourth Gospel: A Narrative Analysis of Their Faith and Understanding*, WUNT 2/290 (Tübingen: Mohr Siebeck, 2010), 135–38; and Jean Zumstein, "The Mother of Jesus and the Beloved Disciple," in Hunt et al., *Character Studies in the Fourth Gospel*, 641–45. Therefore, "from that hour," that is to say, with the arrival and the accomplishment of the fated hour of Jesus, "the disciple took her *into his own home*" (εἰς τὰ ἴδια, 19:27; cf. εἰς τὰ ἴδια, 1:11). See also Schuchard, "Wedding Feast," 103–4, including nn26–30 on 109–10; and the elect lady and her elect sister whose children are those who trust in the testimony of Jesus in 2 John 1, 4, 13, and in Revelation 12:1–17 in Schuchard, *1–3 John*, 615–17, 636–37.

122. Likewise, Koester, *Symbolism*, 203.

123. The sour wine/vinegar (ὄξος) that they offer Jesus in 19:29 (cf. LXX Ps 68:22) he receives in 19:30.

theirs the sweet. He triumphantly declares, "It is finished [τετέλεσται]!" (19:30).[124] And he bows his head and gives up his spirit[125] so those who are his own may receive from him his baptism that is of the Holy Spirit (1:33). He dies. He slumbers. He rests from his labor (cf. Gen 2:2–3), so they with him may awaken to a day that knows no end. From his riven side flows blood and water (19:34).[126] For there can be no baptism of the living water of God that is God's Spirit (3:3; 7:37–39)[127] apart from Jesus's giving up of his spirit (19:30), apart from the shedding of his own blood. There can be no water apart from the blood, no blood apart from the water.[128] The two are inseparable. The Beloved Disciple, the Evangelist, sees and hears these things. He gives witness to them with his writing of the Gospel that bears his name. "His testimony is true. He knows that he tells the truth" (19:35). For his word is the word of the Word Made Flesh, of him who is the Truth.

As evening approaches, and with it the great Sabbath (19:31),[129] the lifeless body of Jesus is taken down from the cross and is prepared for burial. The fallen one is both wittingly and unwittingly honored in fittingly extraordinary terms by Joseph, and by Nicodemus too (19:38–42).[130] And the Day of Preparation (19:14, 31, 42) that was the day of the sacrifice to end all sacrifice and the Passover to end all Passovers finally sees its end.[131]

---

124. Cf. Harold Saxby, for whom the utterance "It is finished!" (τετέλεσται) "unique to John, deliberately links the completion of Christ's earthly ministry with the completion of creation (Gen 2:1)" ("The Time-Scheme in the Gospel of John," *ExpTim* 104 [1992]: 11).

125. See Peter-Ben Smit, "The Gift of the Spirit in John 19:30: A Reconsideration of παρέδωκεν τὸ πνεῦμα," *CBQ* 78 (2016): 447–62.

126. Cf. the Jewish tradition that blood and water flowed from the rock in the wilderness that was struck by Moses in Exod. Rab. 3.13. For the suggestion that "like Adam before him, Jesus sleeps on day six that he might give of his very own flesh for the life of his Beloved, his Bride, that she then might be bone of his bones (cf. 19:36), and flesh of his flesh, that from his riven side the stuff of life might be given," see Schuchard, "Wedding Feast," 104.

127. Likewise, Koester, *Symbolism*, 202–3.

128. See Leopoldo A. Sánchez M., *Receiver, Bearer, and Giver of God's Spirit: Jesus' Life in the Spirit as a Lens for Theology and Life* (Eugene, OR: Pickwick, 2015), 66–69, 191. Contrast the three witnesses of 1 John 5:6–8 in Schuchard, *1–3 John*, 496–544.

129. Cf. the previous day's great Passover.

130. The extraordinary quantity and quality of the spice that they apply to his corpse shows that they do not expect a resurrection "any time soon" (Koester, *Word of Life*, 171). Instead, they offer him a "burial fit for a king" (Koester, *Symbolism*, 228).

131. Cf. 1 Cor 5:7: "For Christ, our Passover Lamb, has been sacrificed."

CHAPTER EIGHT

A DEAD MAN RISES *and* *a* TROUBLED THOMAS

John 20:1–31

I n the story of Jesus that follows, the risen Jesus appears first to Mary. But Mary does not see at first that it is Jesus. Jesus calls her by name. Mary hears the voice of the Good Shepherd (cf. 10:3–5). For the first time Mary sees. She goes to tell the others. But they refuse to believe her. Jesus appears to his disciples. And he breathes on them and says, "Receive the Holy Spirit." By the word of the Word Made Flesh, a final Spirit-wrought sufficiency comes. They come to know him. They see him as finally he must be seen. But Thomas is not with them. So they look for and find Thomas. And they tell him everything. But Thomas refuses to believe them. Jesus appears to Thomas. "Stop refusing to listen!" declares Jesus. Thomas relents and receives and believes and confesses. For they all must believe what they have heard, or never will they see.

In the early-morning (πρωΐ)[1] hours of the first day of the week,[2] a first witness, Mary Magdalene, comes to the tomb. It is still dark (σκοτία).

---

1. For πρωΐ ("early," 20:1; elsewhere only in 18:28) as the last of the four watches of night that would have ended with the rising of the sun, see Mark 13:35. See further Richard Bauckham, "The Horarium of Adam and the Chronology of the Passion," in *The Jewish World around the New Testament: Collected Essays* (Grand Rapids, Baker Academic, 2010), 393–419.

2. In the inclusive scheme that sees the day of the resurrection of Jesus as a "third day" (2:19–20), Jesus dies on the cross Friday afternoon, which is day one, rests in the grave on the "great Sabbath" (19:31), which is day two and the end of the week that was the week of the great and final Passover,

Yet she sees that the stone that was covering the mouth of the tomb has been taken away (20:1).[3] In the darkness of her current understanding of what has transpired, in the darkness of what this means to her now—owned by the darkness—Mary sees but does not see. She sees the evidence of the open tomb but does not see what it means. Instead, she misinterprets everything. And she reports her misunderstanding of what she has seen to Peter and to the Beloved Disciple, saying, "They have taken the Lord out of the tomb, and we do not know where they have laid him" (20:2). She interprets everything that she has seen to mean not that Jesus is risen but that his lifeless corpse has been stolen.[4] In the darkness of her incapacity to understand anything that she sees, every hope that Jesus had previously inspired is, like him, now dead and gone.[5] Mary is distressingly, entirely mistaken.

Second and third witnesses (see Deut 17:6; 19:15; cf. John 8:17), Peter and the Beloved Disciple, go next to the tomb (20:3).[6] They too see a now open tomb. To be sure, they see this and, in the new light of what ought to be seen as a very new day, they see even more. Jesus is gone. But, conspicuously, Jesus's grave clothes (cf. 11:44) are still there. And his face cloth (σουδάριον) is folded and separate in a place by itself (20:4-7).[7] When the Beloved Disciple sees these things, he does a remarkable thing. He is

---

and rises Sunday morning, which is day three and the first day of a *new* week. Counting exclusively, his resurrection is two days later.

3. The text offers again a clear indication of an awareness of standing tradition, here regarding the stone that was placed at the mouth of the tomb (Matt 27:60; Mark 15:46), detail that is not explicitly given but is instead assumed. In other words, the hearer is expected to already know these things. Cf. below the otherwise unexplained "we" in 20:2. While Mary is here featured as an individual who was first to see the open tomb, the hearer is expected to know that she was not alone. Cf. Matthew 28:1; Mark 16:1-2; Luke 23:55–24:1.

4. "Resurrection is not the obvious answer to an open tomb," observes Craig R. Koester, "Therefore, any belief that Jesus has risen and is alive must overcome this alternative explanation of what Mary sees" ("Jesus' Resurrection, the Signs, and the Dynamics of Faith," in *The Resurrection of Jesus in the Gospel of John*, ed. Craig R. Koester and Reimund Bieringer, WUNT 222 [Tubingen: Mohr Siebeck, 2008], 67).

5. Cf. the despair of the disciples on the road to Emmaus in Luke 24:21.

6. The Beloved Disciple arrives first (20:4-5; cf. his believing first in 20:8). Peter enters first (20:6; cf. his coming first to Jesus in 21:7-8 and his dying first in 21:18-23).

7. Contrast Lazarus who is unable to free himself from the bandages of death in 11:44. Andreas Köstenberger observes that all this is "sufficient evidence that the body had not simply been moved." To be sure, it may well suggest that Jesus' body "passed through the linen wrappings very much in the same way as he later was able to appear to his disciples in a locked room." Additionally, "folded" may well mean "that the cloth was still in the exact same position as when Jesus' body had been wrapped

first to believe (πιστεύω) *again* (20:8).⁸ Without seeing anything else the Beloved Disciple interprets the evidence to mean that God has somehow vindicated their master.⁹ Thus, the Beloved Disciple is first to return to his previous understanding of Jesus.¹⁰ The Beloved Disciple's interpretation of the evidence prompts a conclusion that is laudable in that it means that he sees again, and rightly. But, as before, there is also much that he does not yet see. For, as yet, neither he nor the rest of the disciples understand the Scripture¹¹ that Messiah must rise from the dead (20:9).¹² So Peter and the Beloved Disciple return to the others (20:10).¹³ But the news that the two of them share is sorely lacking. For it lacks what they do not yet see.

Mary is again outside the tomb, weeping. She stoops down to see what the others have seen (20:11). But the tomb is no longer empty. There is more for Mary to see. Mary sees two angels (ἄγγελοι; cf. 1:51) in white, sitting suggestively "where the body of Jesus had lain, one at the head and one at the feet" (20:12). And they speak. They ask her, "Woman, why are you weeping?" (20:13). For it is no time for weeping (cf. 11:31, 33; 16:20).

---

in it." In any case, the evidence "rules out grave robbers, who would have acted in haste." Death does not hold him. See *John*, BECNT (Grand Rapids: Baker Academic, 2004), 563–64.

8. Nothing is otherwise said of the reaction of Peter to the same evidence. See, however, Luke 24:12, 24.

9. That the Beloved Disciple concludes that Jesus has been taken by God as was Elijah before him is suggested by Ben Witherington III, *John's Wisdom: A Commentary on the Fourth Gospel* (Louisville: Westminster John Knox, 1995), 325.

10. In fact, as a character in the Gospel the Beloved Disciple seems to consistently enjoy elsewhere a similar credential affirming exceptional and informing prominence. He is, after all, a pillar of the apostolic church (Gal 2:9) and the author of the Fourth Gospel (21:24), the last of the Gospels to be written and, in all likelihood, the last of the works of the New Testament to be written. See Bruce G. Schuchard, *1–3 John*, ConcC (Saint Louis: Concordia, 2012), 1–58. Therefore, he is likely also, like John before him, as close as the Gospel gets to the suggestion of an ideal disciple. First among equals, he is first to become a disciple (1:35–39), first to know the identity of the betrayer (13:23–26), first to enter with Jesus into the courtyard of the high priest (18:15), first to be charged with the care of the household of Jesus (19:26–27), first to arrive at the tomb, first to believe again, and first in the boat to recognize that it is Jesus who is speaking to them from the shore (21:7). Only rarely does Peter precede John. He precedes him in entering into the tomb. He precedes him in coming to Jesus who is on the shore (21:7). He precedes him in joining Jesus in laying down his life for the sheep (21:15–19).

11. If a specific text is in view, Psalm 16:10; Isaiah 53:10–12; and Hosea 6:2 have all been suggested. See also the sign of Jonah in Matthew 12:39–41; 16:4; Luke 11:29–32.

12. For γάρ in 20:9 as possibly "one and the same thing as δέ," meaning either "but" (7:41; 13:29; 20:9) or "now"/"well now" (9:30), see BDAG s.v., γάρ, 2. Therefore, none of them know yet that Jesus is risen.

13. Thus, the referent of "to them" (πρὸς αὐτούς) in 20:10 is the previously mentioned disciples in 20:9 who do not yet know that Jesus must rise from the dead. Cf. the NIV for 20:10, which reads, "Then the disciples went back to where they were staying."

But, again, Mary misinterprets both what she sees and what she hears.[14] She sees but does not see. She hears but does not hear what the angels are intending to suggest. Instead, owned still by the darkness, Mary says for the second time, "They have taken my Lord, and I do not know where they have laid him." Once more, her understanding of what she sees and hears is completely mistaken. She turns and sees someone else. She sees Jesus.[15] But seeing is not believing,[16] nor is it comprehending. So Mary sees but does not see.[17] She does not see that it is he (20:14).[18]

What happens with Mary is what happens when one sees in the dark. The darkness rules and defines. Mary sees but does not see. She hears but does not hear. So when Jesus asks her a question that she has heard before, when he says to her, "Woman, why are you weeping?" (20:15), the point to his word is not heard. The mere repetition of the question first asked by the angels (20:13) accomplishes nothing. Equally ineffectual is Jesus's next question when he suggestively asks, "Whom do you seek?" (cf. 1:38; 18:4, 7).[19] Sadly, Mary fails to see the point to any of Jesus's questions. Instead, Mary speaks a truth that is greater than any of them can possibly know. Still owned by the darkness, Mary thinks that the one standing before her—the Creator of the cosmos (1:3)—is the caretaker (κηπουρός) of the garden that is there. Therefore, for the third time, she sees in what she sees and hears not that Jesus is risen but that his body has been stolen. So, ironically, she says to him, "Sir [κύριε],[20] if you have carried him away, tell me where you have laid him, and I will take him away." Unwittingly hinting at truths throughout, Mary's words show that her understanding of what she sees and hears is woefully mistaken. She

---

14. They are angels, but Mary offers no indication that she is aware of this.

15. Thus, the narrative's heavenly witnesses are also three in number.

16. Likewise, Craig R. Koester, *Symbolism in the Fourth Gospel: Meaning, Mystery, Community*, 2nd ed. (Minneapolis: Fortress, 2003), 68–69.

17. Likewise, Koester, "Jesus' Resurrection," 70.

18. Cf. again the two disciples on the road to Emmaus in Luke 24:15–16.

19. He asks not "what" but "whom." Both in 1:38 and here, "what is found exceeds what is sought," Richard Bauckham, *Gospel of Glory: Major Themes in Johannine Theology* (Grand Rapids: Baker Academic, 2015), 148.

20. That she speaks "better than she knew" is noted by D. A. Carson, *The Gospel according to John*, PNTC (Grand Rapids: Eerdmans, 1991), 636.

sees but does not see. She hears but does not hear. It is Christ alone who sees. It is Christ alone who must now act.

Jesus shows that he knows her. "Mary!" declares Jesus (20:16). He calls her by name (10:3; cf. Lazarus in 11:43) and enlightens her eyes. Turning (20:14; cf. 12:40), Mary hears (10:3–5) and for the first time sees. But there is still much that she does not yet see. There is still much that she and the others do not yet know.[21] So she clings to him (cf. Song 3:4) and will not let go (20:17). She clings to him as though he is here to stay. After all, Messiah abides forever (12:34). And Jesus has previously promised that, returning to them, he will gather them together so that where he is they too may be (14:3). He has promised that he will not leave them as orphans (14:18). But what she and the others do not yet see is precisely what they all must see if any are ever to see.

There is much that they still must know. So Jesus says to Mary, "Stop clinging to me."[22] And the Teacher teaches what only he can teach. "I have not yet ascended to the Father." And, for the first time, Jesus refers to his disciples as his siblings (cf. 1:12). "Go to my *brothers* [ἀδελφούς; cf. 21:23]," declares Jesus, "and say to them that I am ascending to my Father and your Father, to my God and your God." For that is what the arrival and the accomplishment of Jesus's hour has made them. It has made his Father to be their Father (8:35; 14:2–3), his God their God.[23] Mary believes the word of the Word Made Flesh and goes with great joy and excitement. She proclaims to the others, "I have seen the Lord!" (20:18; cf. 20:2, 13, 15). And she tells them *everything* that she has seen and heard. But the disciples refuse to believe her and are instead fearful (20:19; cf. 7:13; 19:38).[24] For, at first, "these words appeared to them as nonsense, and they did not believe [the women]" (Luke 24:11).[25] This, then, initially

---

21. See Christopher Tuckett, "Seeing and Believing in John 20," in *Paul, John, and Apocalyptic Eschatology: Studies in Honor of Martinus C. de Boer*, ed. Jan Krans et al., NovTSup 149 (Leiden: Brill, 2013), 181, citing Bultmann, de Boer, and Koester.

22. For the force here of μή plus the present imperative (here, μή μου ἅπτου) to prohibit an activity that is current and ongoing ("stop"), see James W. Voelz, *Fundamental Greek Grammar*, 2nd ed. (St. Louis, Concordia, 1993), 219.

23. Likewise, Koester, *Symbolism*, 243.

24. "Disciples" appears to include the Beloved Disciple for reasons already specified.

25. Deaf to the first Easter testimony, the disciples were therefore also, at first, just like Mary (see again the two on the road to Emmaus in Luke 24:15–16). Therefore, for good reason they feared what next might come. Cf. Luke 24:36–37. See also, even in the later company of Jesus, who goes to great

the followers all had in common, a persistent inability to see, a distressing unwillingness to hear.

The end of the day and the onset of darkness are near.[26] Darkness threatens to own them still. They have barred the doors where they are for fear of the Jews. And yet Jesus comes. The Good Shepherd is not deterred by a door (10:1–2). The Good Shepherd is the Door (10:7, 9). And so, in spite of their barred doors (20:19), the Good Shepherd comes and stands in their midst to make all things right. And the Word Made Flesh whose word they desperately need to hear speaks. He bespeaks a peace (εἰρήνη) that is not as the world gives but is his alone to give (cf. 14:27). He shows them his hands and his side (20:20). And they grieve and mourn no more. Instead, they rejoice (cf. 16:20–24). Again, he emphatically bespeaks a peace that is his alone to give. And the Sent One sends (20:21). He breathes (ἐμφυσάω) into his disciples the Spirit of Truth (20:22)[27] that he has promised that he and his Father will give (see 14:16–17, 26; 15:26–27; 16:7–8, 12–15). And he charges his sent ones in his stead and by his command to forgive the sins of those who repent and to retain the sins of those who do not (20:23). "Receive the Holy Spirit," declares Jesus. For the Spirit must come and do what Jesus has repeatedly said that Paraclete will do when the Paraclete comes.[28] After the first of these (see 1 John 2:1) must come the second (John 14:16). For they must finally hear with ears that are ready

lengths to reveal himself to them, their unwillingness to believe with their own eyes an experience that to them seems to be too good to be true in Luke 24:41. See further Mark 16:11–14, which states that "when they heard that he was alive and had been seen by her, they would not believe it. After these things he appeared ... to two of them as they were walking into the country. And they went back and told the rest, but they did not believe them. Afterward [Jesus] appeared to the eleven as they were reclining at table, and he rebuked them for their unbelief and hardness of heart, because they had not believed those who saw him after he had risen."

26. If it is still the first day of the week (τῇ μιᾷ σαββάτων) in 20:19 (cf. 20:1), then οὔσης ὀψίας in the same verse refers not to a time after the setting of the sun but just before it. Cf. the use of ὀψία in Matthew 16:2; Mark 1:32; 15:42. See also 6:16.

27. See "he breathed" (ἐνεφύσησεν) here and in LXX Gen 2:7, where God creates man from the dust of the earth and breathes into his face the Breath of Life. (See also LXX 1 Kgs 17:21; Ezek 37:5, 9–10; Wis 15:11; Tob 6:9; 11:11).

28. See especially "But the Paraclete, the Holy Spirit, ... will teach you all things and bring to your remembrance all that I have said to you" (14:26); "But when the Paraclete comes, ... the Spirit of Truth, ... he will bear witness about me" (15:26); "When the Spirit of Truth comes, he will guide you into all truth, ... whatever he hears he will speak, and he will declare to you the things that are to come. He will glorify me, for he will take what is mine and declare it to you" (16:13–14).

to hear.[29] They must finally see what flesh-and-blood eyes can in no way see.[30] They must see Jesus as finally he must be seen.[31]

Jesus imparts to his disciples the Spirit. For everything that they have experienced must finally be seen in terms of what the Word Made Flesh has said or never will they see.[32] By his word alone does a final Spirit-wrought sufficiency come. By word alone is not just the what but also the how and the why of his dying and his rising made known. Only then is it possible for the disciples to see not just that Jesus is risen but that Jesus is *risen and victorious*.[33] Only then is it possible for the disciples to see what flesh-and-blood eyes can in no way see.[34] By word alone of the Word Made Flesh the Spirit does its work. First the Spirit reveals who the Word is. Then the Spirit reveals what the Word has done. Only then do they see one thing, see Jesus, and believe another. Only then is the God no one has ever seen known (1:18).

Only here does the Gospel's story of Jesus explicitly say that the disciple whose Jewish name was Thomas (Θωμᾶς) was "one of the Twelve" (εἷς ἐκ τῶν δώδεκα) (20:24). For the second time it mentions that his Greek name was Didymus (Δίδυμος; see 11:16; see also 21:2).[35] "Now Thomas, one of the Twelve, the one called Didymus, was not with [the Twelve][36] when Jesus came" (20:24). So those Jesus has sent (20:21) look

---

29. Cf. "Then he opened their minds to understand the Scriptures" (Luke 24:45). According to John, he did so by opening their minds by the power of the Spirit of Truth to the significance of his spoken word as an indispensable hermeneutic for their reading of their entire experience of him.

30. "The meaning of Jesus for faith and life remained hidden and unknown until his passion, resurrection, and the coming of the Holy Spirit" (William C. Weinrich, *John 1:1–7:1*, ConcC [St. Louis: Concordia, 2015], 751).

31. See Nicolas Farelly, *The Disciples in the Fourth Gospel: A Narrative Analysis of Their Faith and Understanding*, WUNT 2/290 (Tübingen: Mohr Siebeck, 2010), 174–75, 226–29.

32. Likewise, Koester, *Symbolism*, 69. See also 138–40. Thus, "Jesus' word and his resurrection appearances are tied together in one revelatory event" (William Bonney, *Caused to Believe: The Doubting Thomas Story at the Climax of John's Christological Narrative*, BibInt 62 [Leiden: Brill, 2002], 157. See also 163 and 166).

33. Likewise, Bonney, *Caused to Believe*, 167. See also John Marsh, *Saint John*, WPC (Philadelphia: Westminster, 1968), 647.

34. Weinrich adds, "What opened their eyes was the teaching of Jesus by the power of the Holy Spirit" (*John 1:1–7:1*, 770).

35. Similarly, see J. Ramsey Michaels, *The Gospel of John*, NIBCNT (Peabody, MA: Hendrickson, 1989), 1015. Here and in 11:15, the name Didymus (see also 21:2) helps to frame the Gospel's second half (11:1–20:31).

36. The text here reads "with them" (μετ' αὐτῶν). The referent is the prior "the Twelve" in the same verse. Similarly, Michaels, *John*, 1015. Therefore, what prior context assumes regarding the

for Thomas and find him. But, as before, he whose Jewish and Greek names *both* mean "Twin" is, at first, just like the others were.[37] As before, Thomas refuses to believe what he is hearing. He is once more just like they were.[38] For Thomas completes the picture of what it required and why and what it therefore finally meant for all of them to be reclaimed. He is the last of a dying breed, the last of the disciples to refuse to listen, the last to refuse to believe. Thomas is not, then, a "pessimistic character prone to existential doubt."[39] He is not one who has his doubts and so is not quite sure he can believe what he is hearing. He does not expect or demand proof. Neither then does he attempt to bargain for or to otherwise insist on the experience that the others have had. Instead, Thomas reacts to what he hears from the others in the same way they first reacted. As before, Thomas thinks the others have totally lost their minds.

As before (see "I have seen the Lord" in 20:18), the others say to Thomas, "We have seen the Lord!" (20:25; cf. 20:20). And they tell Thomas *everything*, hoping that he too would receive what they have come to believe. But Thomas is as they were, except as regards one thing. Thomas hears more than the others ever heard from Mary. So Thomas says more. To be sure, what Thomas says grotesquely exceeds anything they have previously said or done. On the one hand, the words "Unless I see in his hands/wrists/forearms [χερσὶν][40] the mark [τύπον] of the nails" might seem to reasonably recall the previous experience of the others (20:20). Even the words "Unless I caste/thrust/drive [βάλω][41] my finger *into* [εἰς] the mark of the nails" one might sanitize so that they too describe

---

previous appearance of Jesus to his disciples in 20:19–23 is here made explicit. He appeared to the Twelve. Cf. "the Eleven" in Luke 24:33.

37. See above the character and significance of Thomas in 11:16 and 14:5.

38. Michaels, *John*, 1016, observes, "The unbelief of one is in some sense the unbelief of all, just as the final confession of faith attributed to just one (see v. 28) belongs finally to them all." Thomas is, then, "the representative disciple" (n46).

39. Köstenberger, *John*, 580. Instead, Köstenberger notes rightly the refusal of Thomas to believe his fellow disciples.

40. See BDAG, s.v. χείρ, 1, which mentions that "the arm may be meant," for the marks of the nails were in all likelihood not in the palms of his hands but were instead in his wrists. See also Koester, *Symbolism*, 207, 212; and Andrew T. Lincoln, *The Gospel according to John*, BNTC 4 (New York: Continuum, 2005), 497.

41. See "to cause to move from one location to another through use of forceful motion" in BDAG, s.v., βάλλω, 1. Thus, Köstenberger, *John*, 578, rightly finds John's choice of a verb "a rather strong term."

little more than what the others were invited to do.[42] But the words of Thomas that follow one cannot easily read in this way. One in fact should not read them in this way. What Thomas says next is patently, is deliberately, hyperbolic. What he says pushes back hard. What they have said to him is preposterous. What they have said is outrageous. So what Thomas says is equally outrageous. "[Unless] I caste/thrust/drive my hand/wrist/forearm into [εἰς] his [riven] side [πλευρὰν]," says Thomas. What Thomas utters is, then, no plausible suggestion of a genuine condition.[43] Instead, Thomas mocks what he has heard. From his perspective, which was previously their perspective, what they have said is impossible. What they have said is absurd.[44] Under no circumstances will Thomas believe it.[45]

For the third time, Jesus must come. For the third time, Jesus must intervene. He comes not because the mere seeing of the risen Jesus is all Thomas needs. Seeing is most certainly not all that is necessary (see Mary in 20:14).[46] In fact, what is necessary has little to do with seeing the risen Jesus. Thomas needs to receive what the others have received, what all must receive if any are ever to see. Thomas must hear what the Spirit has already made it possible for the others to hear. But Thomas refuses to listen. For a week, he does what none may do and live.

---

42. See Jesus' invitation to "touch me" in Luke 24:39.

43. Not all conditional sentences express genuine conditions. See, e.g., "If you are the Son of God" in Matthew 27:40. See also "if" meaning "when" in 1 John 3:2.

44. Not only did Thomas not believe what he was hearing, but he also refuses to take their word seriously. Therefore, his words are "undoubtedly not intended to lay down a serious condition for belief but to expose the absurdity" of what he has been told. "He rejects as impossible the whole idea" (Ridderbos, *John*, 646–47). "He ridicules their claim" with "sarcastic ... incredulity," adds Bonney, *Caused to Believe*, 159. Jesus will later respond with a flat refusal of Thomas's refusal. At the same time, it may also be that Thomas speaks a truth that is greater than he knows. For a τύπος (20:25) is a "mark," a "type," or an "archetype." See BDAG, s.v. τύπος, 6. And the archetypical marks of the Marked One (cf. Rev 5:6, 12; 13:8) are failing to make their mark as all must now be marked (cf. Matt 16:24; Mark 8:34; Luke 9:23; Gal 6:14). "The fact that Jesus continues to bear the signs of his crucifixion is central and significant," observes William C. Weinrich, "The marks of the Crucified characterize the resurrected Jesus and, therefore, reveal how and in what manner the life of the resurrection appears and is lived" ("Doubting 'Doubting Thomas,' " in *The Press of the Text: Biblical Studies in Honor of James W. Voelz*, ed. Andrew H. Bartelt et al. [Eugene, OR: Pickwick, 2017], 264–65).

45. The combination of the double negative and an aorist subjunctive, "is the strongest way to negate something in Greek," which "rules out even the idea as being a possibility." Here, then, οὐ μὴ πιστεύσω means "I will by no means believe" (Daniel B. Wallace, *Greek Grammar beyond the Basics: An Exegetical Syntax of the New Testament* [Grand Rapids: Zondervan, 1996], 468).

46. To see is one thing. To know what you are looking at is another. See further N. T. Wright, *The Resurrection of the Son of God*, COQG 3 (Minneapolis: Fortress, 2003), 23–25, 572–76, who cautions against the notion that, by itself, the resurrection of Jesus "proves" who Jesus is.

A week later (μεθ᾽ ἡμέρας ὀκτώ),[47] on another first day of the week (cf.
20:1, 19), the disciples are again inside (20:26). And Thomas is with them.
Even though they have barred the doors again (cf. 20:19), Jesus comes.[48]
He comes and he stands again in their midst (cf. 20:19). For the third
time Jesus imparts to his disciples a peace that is like no other (cf. 20:19,
21). Turning immediately to Thomas, he who knows all (2:24–25) shows
that he knows what Thomas previously said. In response to the threefold nature of what Thomas has said (20:25), Jesus delivers a threefold
challenge (20:27). First Jesus says, "Bring [φέρε][49] your finger here and
see [ἴδε] my hands/wrists/forearms." Then Jesus says, "Bring your hand/
wrist/forearm and caste/thrust/drive [βάλε] [it] into my side." Finally
Jesus says, "Stop being [μὴ γίνου][50] unbelieving [ἄπιστος]; instead, [be]
believing [πιστός]."[51] He says these things not because the digital explo-
ration of open wounds—a hand/wrist/forearm in the riven side of Jesus—
will settle the matter once and for all. What Thomas needs is not any of
these things. To do any of these things proves little, if that is all that one
does, if that is all that one sees. What is necessary none can empirically
verify. What Thomas needs is *answers* to the questions, how has this happened? and, what does this mean?

---

47. See Köstenberger, *John*, 578. That μεθ᾽ ἡμέρας ὀκτώ (after eight days) is an inclusive expression referring to a day that was "seven days later" is clear from the preposition's use elsewhere with
reference to the day of the resurrection. See "after three days" in Matthew 27:63; Mark 8:31; 9:31; 10:34.
The sys at 20:26 therefore reads, "on the first day of another week" (cf. 20:1, 19). Thus, the Gospel
concludes with a first, second, and third first day of the week in 12:1–2, 20:1 (and 20:19), and here.
The Lord's day (Rev 1:10) is in view. See Carson, *John*, 657. Cf. Barnabas 15:9: "Therefore we celebrate
the eighth day with gladness, for on it Jesus arose from the dead, and appeared, and ascended into
heaven." "Now that the Feast of Unleavened Bread was over, the disciples soon would be returning
home to Galilee (barring instructions to the contrary)," Köstenberger, *John*, 578.

48. "It is as if the earlier scene has been restaged for Thomas's benefit," observes Lincoln, *John*, 502.
"For Thomas' benefit, yes, but for the other disciples' benefit as well," adds Michaels, *John*, 1017n47. "For
this reason, the drama enacted in verses 19–23 is repeated. What was left unfinished is now finished"
(1016).

49. See Michaels, *John*, 1017.

50. Again (cf. 20:17), for the force of μή plus the present imperative (here, μὴ γίνου) to mean
that an activity is to "stop," see Voelz, *Fundamental Greek Grammar*, 219. That γίνομαι here has the
meaning of εἰμί is evident in Codex Bezae (D), which reads μὴ ἴσθι (stop being).

51. "To believe is to renounce unbelief," observes Michaels, *John*, 1017. "There is no middle
ground." Cf. Mark 16:16.

Jesus knows what no ordinary human being is able to know.[52] He responds to Thomas in kind not so Thomas can see and handle and in that way know that Jesus lives and no more. Jesus responds in kind so Thomas will cease and desist, so his foolishness will come to an end.[53] Something else, something supremely necessary because it alone is solely sufficient, must take its place. So Jesus comes. And Jesus speaks. For Jesus can never be seen as he must be seen if Thomas refuses to hear. With the greeting "Peace to you [plural]" on another first day of a very new week, Jesus offers Thomas *everything* that Jesus offered the others exactly as before.[54] For the peace that Jesus has to give he intends for Thomas too. "Stop refusing to listen," implores Jesus. "Stop refusing what the others have received that they are attempting to share." More of what Jesus has previously said he need not now repeat. Thomas has already heard it from them. What Thomas needs to do now is to receive it. He needs to believe it. The challenge is the same as it was for the others. The challenge is the same for all.

Without moving a muscle,[55] Thomas relents and receives and believes what the others have been telling him.[56] By the Spirit of Truth he believes what they have believed. For "no one can say that Jesus is Lord except by the Holy Spirit" (1 Cor 12:3). And Thomas confesses, saying, "My Lord [ὁ κύριός μου] and my God [ὁ θεός μου]" (20:28; cf. 1:1, 14, 18). It may seem that all now is as it should be and that there is little else for Jesus to say or do. But this is not the case. Jesus is not finished. Instead, once more, the Teacher teaches so that the teaching moment for the disciples, including but not limited to Thomas, is not lost. As before, Jesus asks another pedagogically motivated, leading question. "Have you believed

---

52. Likewise, Bonney, *Caused to Believe*, 165. Cf. Nathanael in 1:47–48; and the Samaritan woman in 4:17–19.

53. See Ridderbos, *John*, 647.

54. The "deliberate parallels" in the language of 20:19–23 and 20:24–29 "indicate that the experiences are parallel" (Bonney, *Caused to Believe*, 163). What the others have experienced now Thomas must experience.

55. See Köstenberger, *John*, 579. See further the history of interpretation in Benjamin Schliesser, "To Touch or Not to Touch? Doubting and Touching in John 20:24–29," *Early Christianity* 8 (2017): 69–93.

56. His confession "is best understood as representing the conviction of all the disciples" (Michaels, *John*, 1018).

[πεπίστευκας] because you have seen [ἑώρακας] me?" (20:29).[57] For, in a way, the answer to his question is yes. The seeing precedes. The seeing provokes. The seeing leads to something else. But, in and of itself, does the seeing alone suffice? Does Thomas believe for no other reason than this? Is seeing believing at all?[58] Can it be said that Thomas sees what he believes? Or should it instead be said that Thomas sees one thing and believes another?[59]

Jesus poses a question that invites no simple yes-or-no answer. Instead, like so many of the rest of his questions, this one too—this one especially— is freighted and complex rather than simple. This one requires both a yes and a no from the one who is in the know. For, even now, there are things that the disciples still need to know. In particular—especially now—they need to know that the faithful are *not* those who hold to the conviction of what flesh-and-blood eyes can see.[60] The faithful hold instead to what their eyes can in no way see (Heb 11:1).[61] They do not walk by sight (2 Cor 5:7).[62] With eyes of faith they see (Rom 8:24–25).[63] By the Spirit of Truth in response to the word of the Word Made Flesh, they embrace what remains unseen.[64] Yet such things must still be seen somehow if any are to see Jesus as finally he must be seen. Therefore, "Blessed are those who have not seen and yet have believed," declares Jesus (20:29). The Teacher

---

57. Cf. "Are you believing because" in 1:50, which helps with the phrasing of the same question here to frame and inform the beginning and the end of the Gospel. Both there and here Jesus asks so that he may further inform what they have yet to see.

58. After all, what you see with your eyes you need not believe. What you see is what you know.

59. The suggestion is that of Gregory the Great. See Gregory the Great, *Forty Gospel Homilies*, trans. Dom David Hurst, CS 123 (Kalamazoo, MI: Cistercian Publications, 1990), 207; and Joel C. Elowsky, ed., *John 11–21*, ACCS NT 4b (Downers Grove, IL: InterVarsity, 2007), 373. Cf. Augustine, *Tract. In Evangelium Iohannis Tractatus* 121.5, who suggests that Thomas "saw and touched the man, and acknowledged the God whom he neither saw nor touched."

60. Likewise, Marsh, *Saint John*, 646–49.

61. Cf. 1 Corinthians 13:12, where Paul similarly states, "For now we see in a mirror dimly, but then face-to-face. Now I know in part; then I shall know fully, even as I have been fully known."

62. See also where Paul states that "we look not to the things that are seen but to the things that are unseen, for the things that are seen are transient, but the things that are unseen are eternal" (2 Cor 4:18).

63. What Paul says about hope in Romans 8 applies also. For "hope that is seen is not hope. For who hopes for what he sees?" (8:24). Instead, "we hope for what we do not see" (8:25). "Physical sight is of physical objects. The eye with which a man 'sees'" in Jesus "the one who sent Jesus Christ into the world is not located in any physical body as a sense organ." Instead, the seeing is "distinct from physical sight" (Marsh, *Saint John*, 647).

64. Likewise, Koester, "Jesus' Resurrection," 71–74. Thus, belief "is not the inevitable concomitant of sight." It is instead "the work of the Holy Spirit" (Marsh, *Saint John*, 647).

axiomatically teaches.[65] He describes what is so not just for Thomas and the others but for all who believe.[66] There is more to Jesus than meets the eye. Only ears can tell you what your eyes cannot. So his is a word that must be heard. For the blessed believe what they have heard (Rom 10:17). They take him at his word. With Spirit-wrought eyes they thereby see (9:39; see also Acts 26:18). Only then can they see. Jesus brooks no exceptions. There is no other way. In the end, one takes the Logos at his word or one takes him not at all.[67]

Now Jesus performed many signs (20:30). They were, by definition, signs to be seen with the naked eye. And the performance of them was foundationally necessary. But the signs his followers saw with mere mortal eyes in no way sufficed to inform the unseen. Yet the unseen must still be seen somehow if any are ever to see. The unseen can only be seen by the one who by the Spirit takes to heart and believes the word of the Word Made Flesh. His word, which is the word of his sent ones and so is the word of this book, is alone sufficient to inform what the seeing of Jesus with the naked eye is unable to see.[68] Only his word informs in necessarily final terms what it means for grace to have taken the place of grace (1:16–17).[69] Word alone illumines the final, fulfilling, and completing grace to which the word of the prophets and that of Jesus and his signs pointed.

---

65. See Ridderbos, *John*, 648. See further Wallace, *Greek Grammar*, 562.

66. For Jesus makes plain the true nature of faith. "Faith has no support outside itself; it sees what it sees only in faith," Rudolf Bultmann, *The Gospel of John*, trans. G. R. Beasley-Murray (Oxford: Blackwell, 1971), 232.

67. Marsh, *Saint John*, 647–48, notes that Thomas becomes, then, "the link between the experience of the apostles and that of the later Church, making plain to all believers that there was no advantage to the apostles in 'seeing'; not really, because physical seeing can be as seriously questioned as any other experience of sense; not really, because the vision of Jesus as the Word of God incarnate is the gift of the Spirit both to those who 'see' certain things, and to those who do not. The blessedness of belief is thus really to those who believe, not to those who see. This is the universal beatitude with which John closes his gospel. It includes Thomas as well as contemporary man; and contemporary man as well as Thomas."

68. "What has been eternally spoken has become man for the life of men. What was spoken eternally was spoken by Jesus (Jn 3:32; 8:26, 40, 47) and is continued in the speaking of those sent by him (20:21)" (Weinrich, *John 1:1–7:1*, 129). Thus, one may say that "the Gospel of John is itself the ongoing speaking of the Word through the witness of the Paraclete" and so is "a story that is the definition of God" (128).

69. Marianne Meye Thompson, *John: A Commentary*, NTL (Louisville: Westminster John Knox, 2015), 27. See further above the analysis of 1:16–17.

Many of the signs that Jesus performed in the presence of his disciples "are not written in this book" (20:30; cf. 21:25). But the things (ταῦτα) that are written[70] "stand written" (γέγραπται) (20:31) because the completing counsel of the Word Made Flesh is solely sufficient to inform what must be known if any are ever to see. They stand written so the faithful will steadfastly believe that Jesus is the Christ (ὁ χριστός), the Son of God (ὁ υἱὸς τοῦ θεου), so they may have life (ζωή) in his name (ὄνομα). With such statements the Gospel's story of Jesus comes to an end. But Jesus's end is also a beginning, the beginning of a very new day. With his end comes the beginning of the life and work of his sent ones. More, then, follows. A narrative ends. Another begins. And the focus of the latter is his sent ones. Its focus is the responsibility that Jesus's sent ones will have in the gathering and the care of the sheep of the Shepherd until Jesus comes again.

---

70. The neuter plural nominative demonstrative pronoun ταῦτα in 20:31 refers not to "these [signs]" but to "these things." In other words, ταῦτα refers not to some but to all of the Gospel.

CHAPTER NINE

THE EPILOGUE

John 21:1–25

T he work of Jesus is done. But the work of his sent ones is just beginning. So, once more, there is more that the Teacher must teach them to see. The disciples gather into the net. Then Jesus feeds them. Then Jesus summons them to the pastoral care of the sheep of the Good Shepherd. For the sheep must be fed, fed with the Bread of Life. To follow Jesus is to live from him. To live from him is to live for him until Jesus comes again.

Jesus's work is at an end (cf. "It is finished!" in 19:30). But—in his stead (19:26) and by his command (13:34)—the work of his sent ones (20:21), his apostles (13:16), is just beginning. And so, once more, there is more that the Teacher must teach his disciples to see. For the third time (21:14), Jesus reveals himself again to his disciples,[1] this time by the sea of Tiberias (21:1; cf. 6:1). Seven of his sent ones are together again (21:2). At Peter's instigation (21:3), they return to a work that previously defined them. They get into a boat and go fishing. Jesus, however, has a related but new work in mind for his sent ones (cf. "fishers of men" in Luke 5:1–11). In Jesus, a decidedly new day has dawned for those who are his siblings (20:17), whose brother is the Light of the World. Therefore, "in that night" (ἐκείνῃ τῇ νυκτὶ)—in his absence, in the dark—they "catch"

---

1. The three occasions in view are those in 20:19–23, 20:24–29, and 21:1–14. Every disciple is a follower of Jesus. But, thus far, not every follower of Jesus is one of his disciples. Not every follower will shepherd sheep.

(πιάζω) nothing. But, early in the morning (πρωΐα; cf. 18:28; 20:1), with
its first light and the dawning of a new day, the risen Son, the Light of the
World, appears on the shore (21:4). There is now much that his disciples
know. But there is also still much that they do not yet know. For the lin-
gering influence of the darkness clings to them still. And so, once more,
the disciples see but do not see. They see Jesus standing on the shore but
do not know that it is him.

He who speaks so that they may see speaks again. Jesus addresses his
disciples as the children (παιδία) that they now are (1:11–13; cf. 1 John 2:14,
18; 3:7), who are this in communion with their brother who is God's Son
(20:17). And Jesus teaches what only he can teach when he asks them
another pedagogically motivated, leading question (cf. 1:50; 6:5–6; 20:29).
The Bread of Life (6:35, 48), who gives food (6:55) that is his very own
flesh and his own blood for all the world to eat and drink (6:51–58), puts
them again to the test (cf. 6:6). Jesus asks his disciples if thus far their
experience has left them with "anything to eat" (τι προσφάγιον) (21:5).[2]
Sadly, ironically, their answer is no. So Jesus instructs them to try again
but differently. "Cast the net to the right hand side of the boat," says Jesus,
"and you will find [what I would have you find]" (21:6). His disciples
heed the word of the Word Made Flesh. And, suddenly, their net is so
full of fish that they are unable to bring it into the boat. True to what has
consistently characterized the Beloved Disciple (see 1:35–37; 13:23–26;
19:26–27; 20:2–8), he is first to see rightly that it is Jesus who is speaking with them. And the disciple shares this with Peter (21:7; cf. 13:21–26).
Peter heeds the word of the disciple. And Peter takes up his clothes that
he has laid down (cf. 10:11, 15–18; 13:4, 12; 15:13; 19:23–24),[3] springs into
the sea, and comes first to Jesus (cf. 20:3–6).[4] The others remain in the
boat and follow, dragging with them the net full of fish that is still in the
water (21:8). When the others are out of the boat and on the shore, they

---

2. See BDAG, s.v. προσφάγιον. According to BDAG, the noun refers to a food item, something to
eat, and so is often used with reference to fish (to eat). Therefore, BDAG proposes that here Jesus asks,
"Have you caught anything to eat?" Thus, "the narrative context contrasts the disciples' lack of success
in providing [themselves with] a meal with the Lord's role as chef," as premier provider of food to eat.

3. See also 1 John 3:16. Contrast Peter in 13:37–38 and 21:18–19.

4. "The allusion to Peter's crucifixion later in the chapter (21:18–19) suggests that Peter's actions
on the sea might presage his own death," notes Craig R. Koester, *Symbolism in the Fourth Gospel:
Meaning, Mystery, Community*, 2nd ed. (Minneapolis: Fortress, 2003), 137.

see there a charcoal fire (ἀνθρακιά; cf. Peter in 18:18).[5] On the fire, they see bread and fish (21:9; cf. 6:1–13, esp. vv. 9, 11, 13) prepared for them by him whose bread given for the life of the world is his very own flesh (6:53). Jesus instructs his disciples to bring with them what they have caught (πιάζω) (21:10).[6] Though the fish in the net are large and numerous,[7] none are lost (cf. 6:39; 10:28; 17:12; 18:9). The net holds. It does not tear (21:11; cf. 19:23–24).

The disciples gather (21:6). Jesus feeds (21:9, 12–13).[8] Then Jesus summons his disciples to the pastoral care of the sheep of the Good Shepherd (21:15–17).[9] For the sheep must all be fed, fed with Jesus's bread that is the Bread of Life. The disciples do not endeavor to ask Jesus, "Who are you?" (21:12). They know who he is (21:12). They ask nothing. Instead, he asks. He enlists. He instructs. It is Peter who denied Jesus not once but three times (18:17, 25–27; cf. 13:38). So Jesus shows again that he knows all things (2:24–25). Jesus asks Peter not once but three times, "Do you love me?" (21:15–17). Jesus asks because the time has come for Peter and the others to embrace his example (13:15; 15:9–10, 12–13). The time has come for all of them to follow in his footsteps. It is time for them to lay down their lives too for the sake of the sheep. Not only will Jesus's sent ones talk the same talk. His sent ones will walk the same walk. So Jesus presses his point again and again. Greatly vexed, Peter acknowledges

---

5. "The charcoal fire that Jesus makes on the beach (21:9) is there to remind readers of the one that burned in the courtyard of the high priest (18:18)," Richard Bauckham, *Gospel of Glory: Major Themes in Johannine Theology* (Grand Rapids: Baker Academic, 2015), 147.

6. "The fish the disciples netted were brought to Jesus but not eaten," observes Koester, *Symbolism*, 135. While Jesus "asked Peter to bring him the fish from the great catch," he conspicuously "did not cook any of them. Instead, he invited the disciples to eat what he had already prepared" (136). He invites them to see that what he has prepared is for them ("fish" [ὀψάριον] appears in the Greek of the LXX and New Testament only in 6:9, 11; 21:9, 10 [?], 13). What they have gathered is for him (the term for "fish" common to the rest of the NT [ἰχθύς] appears in the Gospel only in 21:6, 8, 11). For the suggestion that Peter misunderstands Jesus's referent in 21:10, see Bruce G. Schuchard, "The Wedding Feast at Cana and the Christological Monomania of St. John," in *All Theology is Christology: Essays in Honor of David P. Scaer*, ed. Dean O. Wenthe et al. (Fort Wayne, IN: Concordia Theological Seminary Press, 2000), 115n67.

7. For their number, see Andrew T. Lincoln, *The Gospel according to John*, BNTC 4 (New York: Continuum, 2005), 513. See also Koester, *Symbolism*, 312.

8. For the suggestion that the verb ἀριστάω in 20:12 and 15 can refer to "a meal without ref[erence] to a particular time of day or type of food," see BDAG.

9. See especially "Shepherd my sheep!" (ποίμαινε τὰ προβάτιά μου) in 21:16. Cf. Revelation 2:27; 7:17; 12:5; 19:15.

that Jesus truly knows all things. "You know everything!" declares Peter (21:17). Jesus responds so as to make plain, starting with Peter, what the self-sacrificing love of Jesus will require of them all (21:18–19).[10] Jesus summons Peter to the way of the cross, saying, "Follow me" (21:19; see also 20:20, 22; cf. 1:38–39).

With this, the Gospel's story of Jesus and of his sent ones could easily have come to an end. Written from the vantage point of an eyewitness authority speaking in the first-person singular, "I suppose" in 21:25 is a fitting conclusion that compares well with the one in 20:30–31 and follows reasonably after 21:19. What, then, is the purpose of 21:20–24? With these verses the last of the apostles addresses last of all a misunderstanding that too often in his day has contributed to the disillusioned departure of many of Jesus's sheep. Specifically, the apostle addresses an issue arising from something that Jesus also said the day Jesus summoned Peter and the others to lives of cruciform discipleship. With the verses that follow (21:20–24), Peter turns and sees that the Beloved Disciple is near (21:20). So Peter says to Jesus, "Lord, what about this one?" (21:21). Peter asks if his fate (21:19) will also be the fate of the Beloved Disciple. Jesus says to Peter, "If I want him to remain until I come [again], what [is that] to you [τί πρὸς σέ]?" (cf. 2:4). And Jesus emphatically says again to Peter, "Follow me" (21:22). But when Jesus said these things, some failed to comprehend his meaning. "So the saying spread abroad among the brothers that this disciple was not to die" (21:23). But Jesus did not say that the Beloved Disciple would not die. Instead, Jesus said, "If I want him to remain until I come [again], what [is that] to you?"

The epilogue's final verses seek to address a mistaken understanding of Jesus's words that likely contributed to a loss of confidence and the disillusioned departure of many (see 1 John 2:19) when Domitian seized the apostle and exiled him to the island of Patmos (see Rev 1:9).[11] If so, then the impending death of the last of the apostles[12] runs the risk of even greater disillusionment and the painful loss of more of Jesus's sheep. So the apostle adds 21:20–23 here at the end of his Gospel as a needful

---

10. Likewise, Koester, *Symbolism*, 136–37.

11. See again Bruce G. Schuchard, *1–3 John*, ConcC (Saint Louis: Concordia, 2012), 1–58.

12. Late in life, John writes (see Rev 1:11, 19; 2:1, 8, 12, 18; 3:1, 7, 14; 14:13; 19:9; 21:5) because he knows that his days in this world are numbered.

correction of this mistaken understanding of what Jesus previously said. The apostle's contemporaries offer also their own concluding endorsement of the apostle and his work, saying, "This is the disciple who is testifying concerning these things, and who has written these things, and *we* know that his testimony is true" (21:24). "Now there are many other things that Jesus did," adds the apostle, "which, if every one of them were to be written, I suppose that the world itself could not contain the books that would be written" (21:25). And with this the last of the Gospels and, in all likelihood, the last of the works of the New Testament comes to an end.

The Gospel's story comes to an end.

It furthermore awaits an end, an end that is yet to be.

It earnestly awaits an end when all the world will see.

All sightlessness will see its end when then the sightless see.

Just who they are they then will see.

Just as is he they then will be when him they finally see.

And so they all will see the end.

And so will all be at an end when him they finally see.

"Surely, I am coming soon," declares Jesus (Rev 22:20). Blessed brother, dearest friend, come quickly. "The grace of the Lord Jesus be with us all" (Rev 22:21).

BIBLIOGRAPHY

Armbrust, Kevin L. " 'No One Has Ever Seen God' (John 1:18): Not Seeing Yet Believing in the Gospel of John." PhD diss., Concordia Seminary, 2014.

Barrett, Charles K. *The Gospel according to St. John.* 2d ed. Philadelphia: Westminster, 1978.

Bauckham, Richard. *Gospel of Glory: Major Themes in Johannine Theology.* Grand Rapids: Baker Academic, 2015.

———. *The Jewish World around the New Testament.* Grand Rapids, Baker Academic, 2010.

Bennema, Cornelis. *Encountering Jesus: Character Studies in the Gospel of John.* 2d ed. Minneapolis: Fortress, 2014.

Bernard, J. H. *A Critical and Exegetical Commentary on the Gospel of John.* 2 vols. ICC. Edinburgh: T&T Clark, 1928.

Beutler, Johannes. *A Commentary on the Gospel of John.* Translated by Michael Tait. Grand Rapids: Eerdmans, 2017.

Blomberg, Craig. *The Historical Reliability of John's Gospel: Issues and Commentary.* Downers Grove, IL: InterVarsity, 2001.

Bonney, William. *Caused to Believe: The Doubting Thomas Story at the Climax of John's Christological Narrative.* BIS 62. Leiden: Brill, 2002.

Brown, Raymond. *The Gospel according to John.* 2 vols. AB 29–29A. Garden City, NY: Doubleday, 1966–70.

Bultmann, Rudolf. *The Gospel of John.* Translated by G. R. Beasley-Murray. Oxford: Blackwell, 1971.

Caneday, Ardel. "The Word Made Flesh as Mystery Incarnate: Revealing and Concealing Dramatized by Jesus as Portrayed in John's Gospel." *JETS* 60 (2017): 751–65.

Carson, D. A. *The Gospel according to John.* Grand Rapids: InterVarsity, 1991.

Coakley, J. F. "The Anointing at Bethany and the Priority of John." *JBL* 107 (1988): 241–56.

Coloe, Mary L. "The Johannine Pentecost: John 1:19–2.12." *AusBR* 35 (2007): 41–56.

———. "The Mother of Jesus: A Woman Possessed." Pages 202–13 in *Character Studies in the Fourth Gospel: Narrative Approaches to Seventy Figures in John*. Edited by Steven A. Hunt, D. Francois Tolmie, and Ruben Zimmermann, with a foreword by Craig R. Koester. Grand Rapids: Eerdmans, 2013.

———. "The Nazarene King: Pilate's Title as the Key to John's Crucifixion." Pages 839–48 in *The Death of Jesus in the Fourth Gospel*. Edited by Gilbert Van Belle. BETL 200. Louvain: Leuven University Press, 2007.

———. "The Servants/Steward at Cana: The 'Whispering Wizard's' Wine Bearers." Pages 228–32 in *Character Studies in the Fourth Gospel: Narrative Approaches to Seventy Figures in John*. Edited by Steven A. Hunt, D. Francois Tolmie, and Ruben Zimmermann, with a foreword by Craig R. Koester. Grand Rapids: Eerdmans, 2013.

———. "The Woman of Samaria: Her Characterization, Narrative, and Theological Significance." Pages 182–96 in *Characters and Characterization in the Gospel of John*. Edited by Christopher Skinner. LNTS 461. London: Bloomsbury, 2012.

Cullman, Oscar. The *Christology of the New Testament*. Rev. ed. Translated by Shirley C. Guthrie and Charles A. M. Hall. Philadelphia: Westminster, 1963.

Culpepper, R. Alan. *Anatomy of the Fourth Gospel: A Study in Literary Design*. Philadelphia: Fortress, 1983.

Duke, Paul D. *Irony in the Fourth Gospel*. Atlanta: John Knox, 1985.

Elowsky, Joel C., ed. *John 11–21*. ACCS 4b. Downers Grove, IL: InterVarsity, 2007.

Estes, Douglas. *The Questions of Jesus in John: Logic, Rhetoric, and Persuasive Discourse*. BibInt 115. Leiden: Brill, 2013.

Farelly, Nicolas. *The Disciples in the Fourth Gospel: A Narrative Analysis of Their Faith and Understanding*. WUNT 2/290. Tübingen: Mohr Siebeck, 2010.

Fehribach, Adeline. *The Women in the Life of the Bridegroom: A Feminist Historical-Literary Analysis of the Female Characters in the Fourth Gospel*. Collegeville: Liturgical Press, 1998.

Gagne, Jr., Armand J. "An Examination and Possible Explanation of John's Dating of the Crucifixion." Pages 411–20 in *The Death of Jesus in the Fourth Gospel*. Edited by Gilbert Van Belle. BETL 200. Leuven: Leuven University Press, 2007.

Gregory I., Pope. *Forty Gospel Homilies*. Translated by Dom David Hurst. CS 123. Spencer, MA: Cistercian Publications, 1990.

Hylen, Susan. "The Disciples: The 'Now' and the 'Not Yet' of Belief in Jesus." Pages 214–27 in *Character Studies in the Fourth Gospel: Narrative Approaches to Seventy Figures in John*. Edited by Steven A. Hunt, D. Francois Tolmie, and Ruben Zimmermann, with a foreword by Craig R. Koester. Grand Rapids: Eerdmans, 2013.

Keener, Craig S. *The Gospel of John*. 2 vols. Peabody, MA: Hendrickson, 2003.

Koester, Craig R. "Jesus' Resurrection, the Signs, and the Dynamics of Faith." Pages 47–74 in *The Resurrection of Jesus in the Gospel of John*. Edited by Craig R. Koester and Reimund Bieringer. WUNT 222. Tübingen: Mohr Siebeck, 2008.

———. *Symbolism in the Fourth Gospel: Meaning, Mystery, Community*. 2d ed. Minneapolis: Fortress, 2003.

———. *The Word of Life: A Theology of John's Gospel*. Grand Rapids: Eerdmans, 2008.

Köstenberger, Andreas. *John*. BECNT. Grand Rapids: Baker Academic, 2004.

Kruse, Colin G. *The Gospel according to John*. TNTC. Leicester: InterVarsity, 2003.

Luther, Martin. *Sermons on Gospel Texts for Advent, Christmas, and Epiphany*. Vol 1 of *Sermons of Martin Luther*. Edited by John Nicholas Lenker. Translated by John Nicholas Lenker et al. Repr., Grand Rapids: Baker, 1989.

Marsh, John. *Saint John*. WPC. Philadelphia: Westminster, 1968.

Michaels, J. Ramsey. *The Gospel of John*. NIBCNT. Peabody, MA: Hendrickson, 1989.

Miller, Ed. L. "The Johannine Origins of the Johannine Logos." *JBL* 112 (1993): 445–57.

Moloney, Francis J. *John*. SP 4. Collegeville: Liturgical Press, 1998.

Morris, Leon. *The Gospel according to John*. Rev. ed. NICNT. Grand Rapids: Eerdmans, 1995.

O'Brien, Kelli S. "Written That You May Believe: John 20 and Narrative Rhetoric." *CBQ* 67 (2005): 284–302.

O'Day, Gail R. *Revelation in the Fourth Gospel: Narrative Mode and Theological Claim*. Philadelphia: Fortress, 1986.

Porter, Stanley E. *John, His Gospel, and Jesus: In Pursuit of the Johannine Voice*. Grand Rapids: Eerdmans, 2015.

———. *Sacred Tradition in the New Testament: Tracing Old Testament Themes in the Gospels and Epistles*. With a chapter by Bryan R. Dyer. Grand Rapids: Baker Academic, 2016.

Ridderbos, Herman. *The Gospel of John: A Theological Commentary*. Translated by John Vriend. Grand Rapids: Eerdmans, 1997.

Rissi, Mathias. "Die Hochzeit in Kana (Joh 2,1–11)." Pages 76–92 in *Oikonomia: Heilsgeschichte als Thema der Theologie. Oscar Cullmann zum 65. Geburtstag*. Edited by Felix Christ. Hamburg: Reich, 1967.

Sánchez M., Leopoldo A. *Receiver, Bearer, and Giver of God's Spirit: Jesus' Life in the Spirit as a Lens for Theology and Life*. Eugene, OR: Pickwick, 2015.

Saxby, Harold. "The Time-Scheme in the Gospel of John." *ExpTim* 104 (1992): 9–13.

Schlatter, Adolf. *Der Evangelist Johannes*. 2d ed. Stuttgart: Calwer, 1948.

Schliesser, Benjamin. "To Touch or Not to Touch? Doubting and Touching in John 20:24–29." *Early Christianity* 8 (2017): 69–93.

Schuchard, Bruce G. *1–3 John*. ConcC. Saint Louis: Concordia, 2012.

———. "Form versus Function: Citation Technique and Authorial Intention in the Gospel of John." Pages 23–45 in *Abiding Words: The Use of Scripture in the Gospel of John*. Edited by Alicia D. Myers and Bruce G. Schuchard. RBS 81. Atlanta: SBL Press, 2015.

———. "The Gospel of John and the Word of the Word-Made-Flesh." *Didaktikos* 1 (January 2018): 45.

———. *Scripture within Scripture: The Interrelationship of Form and Function in the Explicit Old Testament Citations in the Gospel of John*. SBLDS 133. Atlanta: Scholars Press, 1992.

———. "Temple, Festivals, and Scripture in the Gospel of John." Pages 381–95 in *The Oxford Handbook of Johannine Studies*. Edited by Judith M. Lieu and Martinus C. de Boer. OHS. Oxford: Oxford University Press, 2018).

———. " 'That They May Be One': Lutheran Interpretation of John 17 from the Reformation to Today." Pages 83–98 in *Lutheran Catholicity*. Edited by John A. Maxfield. The Pieper Lectures 5. St. Louis: Concordia Historical Institute and the Luther Academy, 2001.

———. "The Thursday Evening and Friday Morning and Afternoon That Was the Passover: The Chronology of the Passion in the Gospel according to John." Pages XXX in *One of the Holy Trinity Suffered for Us: Essays in Honor of Dr. William C. Weinrich*. Edited by James Bushur. St. Louis: Luther Academy, forthcoming.

———. "The Wedding Feast at Cana and the Christological Monomania of St. John." Pages 101–16 in *All Theology is Christology: Essays in Honor of David P. Scaer*. Edited by Dean O. Wenthe, William C. Weinrich, Arthur A. Just Jr., Daniel Gard, and Thomas L. Olson. Fort Wayne, IN: Concordia Theological Seminary Press, 2000).

Smit, Peter-Ben. "The Gift of the Spirit in John 19:30: A Reconsideration of παρέδωκεν τὸ πνεῦμα." *CBQ* 78 (2016): 447–62.

Smith, D. Moody. *John*. ANTC. Nashville: Abingdon, 1999.

Stibbe, Mark W. G. *John as Storyteller: Narrative Criticism and the Fourth Gospel*. SNTSMS 73. Cambridge: Cambridge University Press, 1992.

Talbert, Charles H. *Reading John: A Literary and Theological Commentary on the Fourth Gospel and the Johannine Epistles*. Reading the New Testament. New York: Crossroad, 1992.

Thompson, Marianne Meye. *The God of the Gospel of John*. Grand Rapids: Eerdmans, 2001.

———. *John: A Commentary*. NTL. Louisville: Westminster John Knox, 2015.

Tuckett, Christopher. "Seeing and Believing in John 20." Pages 169–85 in *Paul, John, and Apocalyptic Eschatology: Studies in Honor of Martinus C. de Boer*. Edited by Jan Krans, Bert Jan Lietaert Peerbolt, Peter-Ben Smit, and Arie Zwiep. NovTSup 149. Leiden: Brill, 2013.

Voelz, James W. *Fundamental Greek Grammar*. 2d ed. St. Louis, Concordia, 1993.

Wallace, Daniel B. *Greek Grammar beyond the Basics: An Exegetical Syntax of the New Testament*. Grand Rapids: Zondervan, 1996.

Weinrich, William C. "Doubting 'Doubting Thomas.' " Pages 254–69 in *The Press of the Text: Biblical Studies in Honor of James W. Voelz*. Edited by Andrew H. Bartelt, Jeffrey Kloha, and Paul R. Raabe. Eugene, OR: Pickwick, 2017.

———. *John 1:1–7:1*. ConcC. St. Louis: Concordia, 2015.

Westcott, Brooke F. *The Gospel according to St. John: The Greek Text with Introduction and Notes*. 2 vols. London: Murray, 1908.

Whitacre, Rodney A. *John*. NTC 4. Downers Grove, IL: InterVarsity, 1999.

Witherington, III, Ben. *John's Wisdom: A Commentary on the Fourth Gospel*. Louisville: Wesminster John Knox, 1995.

Wilckens, Ulrich. *Das Evangelium nach Johannes*. NTD 4. 17th ed. Göttingen:Vandenhoeck & Ruprecht, 1998.

Williams, Catrin H. "John (the Baptist): The Witness on the Threshold." Pages 45–60 in *Character Studies in the Fourth Gospel: Narrative Approaches to Seventy Figures in John*. Edited by Steven A. Hunt, D. Francois Tolmie, and Ruben Zimmermann, with a foreword by Craig R. Koester. Grand Rapids: Eerdmans, 2013.

Wright, N. T. *The Resurrection of the Son of God*. COQG 3. Minneapolis: Fortress, 2003.

Zumstein, Jean. "The Mother of Jesus and the Beloved Disciple." Pages 641–45 in *Character Studies in the Fourth Gospel: Narrative Approaches to Seventy Figures in John*. Edited by Steven A. Hunt, D. Francois Tolmie, and Ruben Zimmermann, with a foreword by Craig R. Koester. Grand Rapids: Eerdmans, 2013.

SUBJECT INDEX

A

Abraham, 10nn31 and 34, 24n74, 26, 38n2, 48–50, 81n24

Adam, 10n36, 33n38, 41n20, 51n66, 55n94, 99n126, 101n1

afternoon, 68n5, 101n2. *See also* morning; evening

Andrew, 16, 16n19

Annas, 93–94

anoint(ing). *See* foot; fragrance

anticipate, 6, 8, 13, 13n2, 15, 15n15, 19–20, 25, 37, 49n52, 51, 59n1, 63n21, 67, 75, 88n66, 89. *See also* foreshadow

apostle, 19n33, 38n6, 80, 113n67, 115, 118–119. *See also* send

B

baptism(al), 15, 19, 99. *See also* bath; clean

(John the) Baptist, 6, 8, 8n20, 13–16, 25, 34, 37, 57–58

bath, wash, 19, 27n9, 30n26, 51–52, 72n27, 79, 79nn12, 14, 16, and 17. *See also* baptism; clean

Beloved Disciple, 16n19, 43n29, 80–81, 93–94, 97–99, 102–3, 105n24, 116, 118

betray, betrayal, betrayer, 16n17, 68n2, 79–81, 87, 92, 92n93, 103n10. *See also* Judas

blasphemy, blaspheme, 33, 48n50, 56–57

blind, blindness, sightless, 7, 10–11, 22, 28, 30, 37, 41n22, 46, 50–53, 55, 64, 74, 74n38, 119. *See also* eye(s)

blood, 7, 11, 15, 19, 19n39, 21, 33n41, 41nn19 and 21, 45n37, 72n27, 99, 99n126, 107, 112, 116

Booths, Feast of. *See* feast

born, 18, 21n50, 22, 22nn60 and 62, 38n5, 50n56, 95

bread, 19n33, 21n48, 26n5, 27n9, 31n27, 38–42, 81, 81n25, 94n106, 110n47, 115–17. *See also* fish

bride, wife, 20–21, 38nn5–6, 69n14, 70, 71n21, 99n126, 31n27, 38n6. *See also* mother; woman

bridegroom, husband, 6, 6n8, 19, 19n39, 26, 26nn2 and 5, 28, 31n27, 69, 69nn10 and 14, 71n21

brother, 8n19, 16, 38n2, 42n23, 43, 43n29, 45n36, 59, 61–63, 82n35, 98n120, 105, 115–16, 118–19.

C

Caiaphas, 65, 93–94

clean(se), purify, purification, 15, 19, 19nn36 and 39, 20n42 79, 79nn14 and 16, 80n21,

thirty-eight, 30–31
fifty, 49

O

ointment. *See* foot; fragrance

P

Paraclete, 77, 83–85, 87–88, 106,
106n28, 113n68
(Feast of the) Passover. *See* feast
perfume. *See* fragrance
Peter, 16, 16n19, 42, 43n28, 45n38,
61nn9–10, 79, 79nn14–16,
81–82, 92n94, 93–94, 99n125,
102–3, 115–18
Pharisees, 22, 22n56, 25, 46, 52n71, 53,
64, 72, 92
Philip, 16–18, 83, 83n39
Pilate, 17n25, 86n59, 94–97
priest(s), 19n40, 44n31, 46, 54n78,
64, 70n16, 72, 91n82, 92–94,
97, 103n10, 117n5
Preparation, Day of, 20n45, 97,
97n116, 99. *See also* Sabbath;
week
prophet(s), 10n33, 16, 17n26, 19n39,
21n52, 26, 28–29, 31, 31n27, 39,
39n8, 42n23, 45–49, 53, 53n73,
74n38, 88n66, 113
purify, purification. *See* clean

R

rabbi(s), 17n26, 22, 62n16, 69n10. *See
also* teach(er)
reality, truth, 8–10, 15, 19n38, 33n41,
41n22, 45n36, 87
representative character(s), 22n57,
26–27, 31n27, 56n99, 59, 61,
61nn11–12, 80, 82–84, 93, 108,
108n38–39, 111n56. *See also*
Thomas, Twin

S

Sabbath, 31–33, 52, 68, 68nn4–5, 97,
97nn115–116, 99, 101n2. *See
also* Preparation; week
sacrifice, 10n31, 20–21, 38n2, 44n31,
70–71, 79n17, 97–99, 118.
See also Lamb, Feast of the
Passover
Samaritan(s), 22n62, 25–29, 31n27,
38n5, 48, 53, 61n9, 68n3,
111n52
send, sender, sent one, 2, 5, 11, 23,
33n42, 34n48, 47n43, 51–52,
57n103, 80, 80n19, 85, 85n48,
98, 113–15, 117–18. *See also*
apostle
servant, suffering servant, 5n1, 14n9,
15n12, 18, 19n33, 30, 45n36, 48,
79–80, 82n35, 86
sheep, 26n5, 30, 30nn25–26, 39n11,
54–56, 90n78, 94n103, 98,
103n10, 114–15, 117–18
shepherd, 19n40, 30n25, 37, 54–56, 59,
64, 71n21, 78n9, 79n17, 90n78,
94n103, 98, 101, 106, 114–15,
117, 117n9
Speech, 1–3, 9, 9n29, 57
sufficient, 2, 15–16, 29, 34, 37, 40, 53,
58, 67, 75, 101, 102n7, 107, 111,
113–14. *See also* necessary
sunrise, 94, 94n107, 101n1. *See also*
morning
sunset, sundown, 40n17, 68, 68n4,
106n26. *See also* afternoon;
evening
supper. *See* meal
symbol(ism), 17n22, 20n42, 79n14,
80n21
synagogue, 50n56
Synoptic Gospels, 14n4, 68n2

T

Tabernacle, Tent of Meeting, 8n17,
70n16, 71n24. *See also* temple

SCRIPTURE INDEX

Old Testament

Deuterocanonical Books

Pseudepigrapha

Ancient Jewish Writers

New Testament

Rabbinic Works

Early Christian Writings

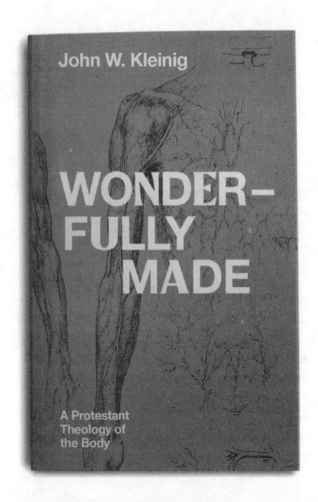

John W. Kleinig

WONDER–FULLY MADE

A Protestant
Theology of
the Body

ALSO AVAILABLE
FROM LEXHAM PRESS

Think deeply about God's word and the body

——

Visit lexhampress.com to learn more